C000040463

HALF-DAY WALKS
in
THE PEAK DISTRICT:
The South West

Alan Bradley

Copyright © A.C. Bradley, 1996

All Rights Reserved. No part of this publication may be reproduced, stored in a retrieval system, or transmitted in any form or by any means – electronic, mechanical, photocopying, recording, or otherwise – without prior written permission from the publisher.

Published by Sigma Leisure – an imprint of Sigma Press, 1 South Oak Lane, Wilmslow, Cheshire SK9 6AR, England.

British Library Cataloguing in Publication Data
A CIP record for this book is available from the British Library.

ISBN: 1-85058-438-9

Typesetting and Design by: Sigma Press, Wilmslow, Cheshire.

Cover photograph: Shutlingsloe from Shining Tor *(Alan Bradley)*

Photographs: The author

Sketches: Elma Bradley

Maps: The author

Printed by: MFP Design & Print

Disclaimer: the information in this book is given in good faith and is believed to be correct at the time of publication. No responsibility is accepted by either the author or publisher for errors or omissions, or for any loss or injury howsoever caused. Only you can judge your own fitness, competence and experience.

PREFACE

There are many guides to footpaths in the Peak District. Why another? What is different about this book is that all the walks are short; three to five miles (apart from one easy six-mile walk), easily completed in half a day. They will suit those with small children, those with little time to spare, and those who are feeling older or are just plain lazy. None of the walks duplicates those to be found in the most popular half-dozen footpath guides, so this book supplements those guides rather than replacing them. I hope it will introduce even those who know the Peak to some unfamiliar but enjoyable places.

The walks in this volume are in the south-west part of the Peak, defined for this purpose as west of the A515 road which crosses the Peak District National Park from Buxton to Ashbourne. Most are entirely within the Peak Park though a few stray outside it.

All the walks are circular, returning you to your car without retracing your steps for more than a short distance, except one where the loop is completed by a regular train service. Public transport is scarce in this part of the Peak Park, but where it exists it is mentioned.

Other features of the book are clear sketch maps to supplement the route descriptions; a choice of starting points (with safe parking) for most walks, to suit those coming from different directions; and alternative routes, some shorter but most a little longer, for those who have more time or have done the walk before and would like a change.

There are comments on the suitability of each route for poor weather, and a description of features of interest and of facilities, including public toilets, and cafes and pubs which serve good hot food at lunchtime.

Nearly all of these walks I have taken over the past two or three years with my wife Elma. On some of them we have been accompanied by friends. I thank all of them for their company.

Alan Bradley

CONTENTS

The Walks

Distances are shown in miles, for the main route and (in parentheses) for the alternatives. One mile = 1.6 kilometres.

The Goyt area

The Dane and Churnet area

The Manifold and Hamps area

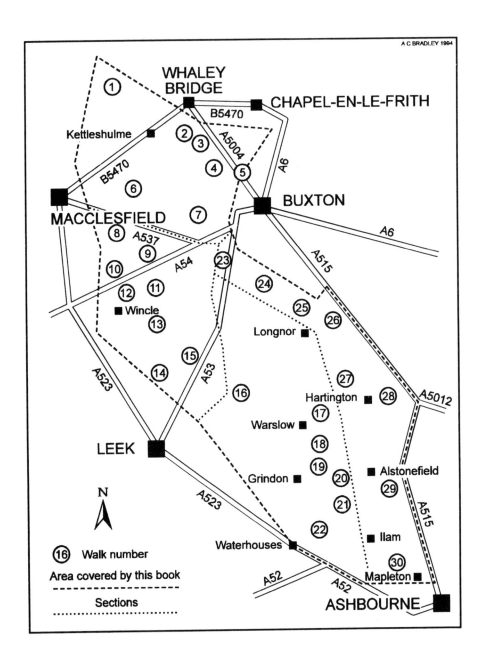

INTRODUCTION

The Peak District

The Peak District, which occupies the southern tip of the Pennines, is one of the finest of the National Parks for weekend walking. It is also the most popular, surrounded as it is by cities and industrial towns; and yet it consists mostly of quiet, unspoilt countryside, despite the intrusion of a few large quarries and the many traces of past industry. The most popular areas, such as Dovedale, can become overcrowded at summer weekends, though quiet enough at other times. To some extent, erosion and the measures taken to combat it have detracted from their beauty. But there are plenty of unspoilt areas which are just as attractive to the walker, both in the limestone country of the 'White Peak' and among the high gritstone moors of the 'Dark Peak' that surround the limestone like a horseshoe. I hope this book will introduce you to some of these places.

For those who do not know the area, do not expect mountains. The name 'Peak' has nothing to do with the landscape but comes from the name of a tribe that lived here in prehistoric times. Instead you will find open moorland and steep rocky valleys or 'dales', but also much farmland and many villages; the Peak has a larger population than most of the other National Parks.

These walks are in the south-west part of the Peak. I have chosen, as an arbitrary but convenient boundary, the A515 road which crosses the Peak District National Park from Buxton to Ashbourne. Most of the walks are entirely within the Peak Park though a few stray outside it, divided fairly equally between Cheshire, Staffordshire and Derbyshire. Strangers are sometimes surprised to find that the Peak Park is not entirely in Derbyshire. In fact parts of it fall in Staffordshire, Cheshire, Greater Manchester, West Yorkshire and South Yorkshire. Even Dovedale, the most famous of the 'Derbyshire Dales', is half in Staffordshire; the river Dove is the county boundary from its source on Axe Edge all the way to its departure from the Park near Ashbourne.

My boundary, the A515 Buxton to Ashbourne road, runs approximately along the watershed between the valley of the Dove and those of the Wye, Lathkill and Derwent which can be regarded as forming the south-east Peak. For convenience I have subdivided the list of walks into four areas corresponding to the valleys of the Goyt, with the ridge to the west of it; the Dane and Churnet; the Manifold and Hamps; and the Dove, all with their various tributaries. Of these rivers the first two drain into the Mersey and the Irish Sea, while the others join near the southern boundary of the park and run into the Trent and eventually the North Sea. So the ridge of Axe Edge and the Morridge, which separates these two groups, is the main watershed of the south Peak District.

The Goyt section covers the tip of the western salient of the Park, roughly north of the A537 road from Buxton to Macclesfield. Dane and Churnet is south of this and west of the Axe Edge – Morridge ridge, which runs not far from the A53 Buxton to Leek road. The other two sections are separated by the long spur, carrying only minor roads, which runs from Axe Edge through Longnor, Sheen, and Alstonefield to end spectacularly in Bunster Hill above the mouth of Dovedale.

The National Park

The Peak District National Park is administered by the Peak Park Planning Board, based in Bakewell which is the Park's only town. I probably need not remind readers that national parks in the UK, unlike many of those abroad, are not owned by the nation. Ownership of the land remains with the farmers and other landowners, and the authorities have the task of balancing the interests of the residents with those of the many visitors. Much of their work goes on 'behind the scenes' and will not be apparent to visitors, but the more public aspects include maintenance of car parks and footpaths and the running of information centres. They publish a very useful annual broadsheet, 'Peakland Post', which is available free from all information centres within the Park and many outside it. This includes details of the opening times and charges of most of the tourist attractions and information centres in the Park, and also a calendar of events within or near the Park including such attractions as well-dressings, carnivals, sheepdog trials and guided walks.

One activity of the Park authorities which is very visible is the conversion of abandoned railway lines into firm paths for walkers, cyclists and horse riders. There are several of these 'trails'; two are entirely within the area covered by this book. One is the 'Manifold Way', which starts on the southern boundary of the Park near Waterhouses and runs down the Hamps valley, and then up the Manifold valley, to a terminus at Hulme End south-west of Hartington. The other is the 'Tissington Trail' which enters the park near Ashbourne and converges with the 'High

Peak Trail' at Parsley Hay north of Hartington. The walkable part of the 'High Peak Trail' is mostly to the east of our area, but we do have the part from Parsley Hay north for a few miles to Sparklow, beyond which the line is still in use for mineral traffic; and there are other walkable stretches in the Goyt Valley. Walks along the trails are covered by various books and leaflets so I shall not repeat them here, but short sections of the trails are used in some of the walks.

Readers who want a change from walking may like to know that the Board also runs cycle hire centres, three of which serve the area covered by this volume; they are at Parsley Hay near Hartington on the 'High Peak Trail', at Waterhouses at the southern end of the 'Manifold Way', and at Ashbourne at the south end of the 'Tissington Trail'. The latter two are actually just outside the Park boundary.

I have pointed out that the land in the Park is privately owned. There are exceptions to this: some of the more interesting parts are owned by the National Trust, the Peak Park Planning Board, and other bodies which encourage public access. They may still require you to keep to established paths, so that part of their land can serve as an undisturbed nature reserve. In addition, some of the moors have (by agreement with the landowners) been designated 'Access land' where the public can walk at will. Most of this access land, however, is in the northern and eastern parts of the Park and so not covered by this book.

Guidebooks

Peakland walks have been made better known by many footpath guides which have been published in the last twenty years. Among the best of these are 'East Cheshire Walks' and the 'Pub Walks' series from Sigma Press, an excellent set of three books by Mark Richards, a book of weekend walks by John and Ann Nuttall (all these from Cicerone Press), and two slim 'Family Walks' books by Norman Taylor from Scarthin Books. But all of these, except the last, concentrate on longer walks. In this book I have collected walks which suit those of us who prefer shorter walks because of our age or that of our children, or who are short of time, or just lazy. I have taken care not to duplicate any of the walks included in the books I have mentioned, although of course there is bound to be some overlap. If you find my walks match those in other books which I have not read, my apologies to readers and my congratulations to the authors on choosing the best routes!

The Landscape

About a third of the area covered by the book, and a similar proportion of the walks described, are on the limestone of the 'White Peak'. The rest of the area includes the gritstone of the 'Dark Peak' and the softer shale separating the two, which provides routes for some of the Peak-land rivers. These walks give you the opportunity to compare the contrasting landscapes associated with the three types of rock, so I shall give a very brief account of these landscapes.

The limestone country is mainly an undulating plateau cut into by steep valleys, or dales. These are often rocky and sometimes dry, with short grass and scrub or woodland. The plateau itself is farmed, almost entirely as pasture, with few trees other than shelter belts to protect farmhouses. Walls are of white or pale grey limestone. The soil drains well and is usually reasonable for walking even after rain, though where the rock is exposed it can be slippery. Limestone is a valuable mineral and great quarries scar some parts of the White Peak, though most of the areas where quarrying is still active are excluded from the National Park. Smaller quarries, long disused, exist in their hundreds. Some of these were for lime for burning to improve the soil, or for use in mortar; usually the ruins of a kiln can be seen very near by. Others were for building stone for walls or houses. Limestone is soft and not ideal for building, so often millstone grit has been brought from the surrounding areas for window and door surrounds and for the corners of buildings. In the past these limestone areas have also produced lead and copper. The mines are now all closed, though in one or two places the mined ground is being re-worked for other minerals. Limestone is porous (geologists, please forgive me for this simplification) and the streams often find their way underground, leaving the valleys dry. It is limestone that forms the famous Dales – including Dovedale, Wolfscote Dale and Beresford Dale in our area, and others elsewhere in the White Peak – and the famous caves of Buxton (just outside the area covered by this book) and Castleton.

Millstone grit, a coarse sandstone, underlies the high moors. These are often peaty and usually covered by heather or by coarse grass with rushes in the wetter patches, except where the land has been improved for use as pasture; the going can be wet at times. In places there are crags and cliffs, although these are more common in the eastern part of the Peak District. There are small quarries, almost all now closed. Most were for building stone, though a few produced millstones – but millstone quarrying is much better seen in the east of the Peak District. There has also been small-scale mining of coal in a few places; this too ceased as soon as better coal could be brought to the Peak by rail and road. But another resource of the gritstone area is still very much in demand – water; the rock is impervious and so the deeper valleys are ideal sites for reservoirs. There are a few of these in our area, most notably in the Goyt Valley; many more in the north and east of the Peak.

Some of this gritstone area is farmed, and there are patches of reasonable pasture near the farms; a great deal of effort in drainage and soil treatment (especially with lime) has gone into these patches. Much more of the land has been enclosed and to some extent improved in the past, but has been allowed to revert with the walls broken and the barns and farms ruined. This land is fit only for sheep, and not very welcoming even for them (but do drive carefully – sheep are singularly lacking in road sense). The heather moors are useful only for grouse shooting, and were once jealously preserved from ramblers for this reason. Fortunately much of this land is now open to the walker; a story in itself, but not one I can tell here. Some moors are closed for a few days (never Sundays) in the autumn for shooting, but even here any rights of way remain open; and once you've tried walking through thick heather, you'll soon see the point of sticking to trodden paths. Walls in gritstone country are fewer, and are of brown gritstone which is often blackened by exposure. Often the clearest indication that you are crossing the boundary between gritstone and limestone is a change in the colour of the field walls, because walling stone was never carried far.

In between the limestone and gritstone rocks lie the less extensive shales. These are softer and produce a gentle and reasonably fertile landscape, so practically all the areas of shale are farmed. Nowadays livestock farming predominates, but in places there is evidence of arable farming in earlier days. Because the shale is soft it forms an easy course for rivers, and in particular the upper course of the Dove is along a broad straight band of shale that forms the boundary between the White Peak and the Dark Peak. Shale is useless as a building stone, so gritstone or limestone is brought from elsewhere; walls are often replaced by hedges or fences.

The only town within the Park (though not in the area of this book) is Bakewell, a small market town which caters for tourists without going

overboard about them. Buxton, a larger town and former spa, was deliberately excluded from the park; Matlock, the seat of Derbyshire County Council, lies just outside it to the south-east. The villages of the Peak are mostly rural and attractive. Few of those within the area covered by this book are of any size, as judged by their ability to support more than one pub. The largest is probably Hartington, which has become something of a tourist centre, rather to its detriment, and also has a successful cheese factory. Other multi-pub villages are Longnor, also popular with tourists but not overwhelmed by them, and Kettleshulme near the northern tip of the area which is well off the tourist beat. Several other villages cater for tourists to the extent of having a car park and sometimes a toilet block, but tourism is clearly not the major industry in any of these.

Peak district buildings are mostly in the local limestone or gritstone, thanks to the planning control exercised by the Peak Park board, and blend well with the landscape. There is less control over farm buildings, and these sometimes intrude, though there are only a few of the tall silo towers. Stone walls are very much a feature of the park, and while some are disused and derelict, most are well maintained. Besides the lie of the land itself, it is buildings, walls and trees that create the characteristic landscape of the Peak.

The Walks

Most of the walks in this book are between three and five miles in length, although they may include a fair amount of ascent and descent. One is a mile longer, but over easier country. In all cases two to three hours (plus any stops) should be enough for the average to slow walker. I have tried to distinguish between walks which need dry weather and those which are passable even after rain, though I have not walked every route in every season. Conditions in this part of the Peak do not compare with those on the northern moors, but rain can come unexpectedly and the winter wind can be very cold. In winter I would certainly recommend boots for most of these walks, because muddy patches are unavoidable. There should be no need for compass, whistle and survival bag; but don't forget your waterproofs and a warm jumper – and the thermos if you are one of those who need tea or coffee to keep you going.

I have mentioned that grouse moors may occasionally be closed for shooting in the autumn, though this does not affect rights of way. In very dry weather it is occasionally necessary to close some areas of moor because of fire or the risk of it. Very occasionally, the authorities have had to ban or at least discourage walking in some areas – particularly farmland – because of animal diseases such as foot-and-mouth. If you come across such restrictions, please observe them – your short cut may make the difference between life and death for a whole herd of cattle.

Nearly all of these walks I have taken over the past two or three years with my wife Elma, for exercise and enjoyment rather than as a basis for writing. We have walked at all times of year; perhaps more in autumn, winter and spring than in the summer, when holidays tend to take us elsewhere. The Peak is beautiful at all times, but my own view is that much of it – especially the gritstone moorland – is at its best in the 'off-season', when the leaves are off the trees. Best of all are those winter days when snow offsets the darkness of the rock, or hoar frost ices every tree and blade of grass, and mud is turned rock-solid.

Maps

I have included a sketch map of each walk. These vary slightly in scale, and occasionally in orientation, to fit them on the page; but in all cases the scale and north point are clearly shown. I have shown roads and relevant car parks, and have distinguished between the main route and alternative routes described in the text. Other paths (not necessarily rights of way), and details such as buildings and woods, are shown only where relevant to route finding. I have not shown walls and fences; there are so many that the map would be very cluttered by them. Nor have I shown bridges or stepping stones. You can take it for granted that where the route crosses water, there is a dry way across: if there may be problems in wet weather, the text will say so. In places I have distorted the scale to show details more clearly (incidentally, all distances in the text are approximate). The maps are intended to supplement the text rather than replace it, and to help you find the starting point and relate the route to Ordnance Survey maps.

With these sketch maps and the text there should be no difficulty in following the route. Nevertheless I strongly recommend that you carry a good map, preferably the Ordnance Survey Outdoor Leisure 'White Peak' map at a scale of 1 to 25000 (about 2½ inches to the mile). This will not only let you make your own variations on the routes I give, perhaps to suit a different parking spot or to make the walk longer or shorter; it will also tell you a great deal about your surroundings, and in particular the contours will show you the relief of the countryside. The great merit of this map for walkers is that it shows field boundaries, essential if you are following a path without a detailed guide. Don't forget that a path shown as a right of way may be impassable in practice, though it certainly ought not to be. One word of advice: this is a double-sided map, and it is almost impossible to reverse it in a high wind – difficult enough in a car. So make sure it is right way round before you leave home. Practically all of the walks in this volume are on the 'western' side of the sheet. A couple of walks are just outside (or partly outside) this map; the details in this book will enable you to find your way, but I shall point out which of the 1:25000 'Pathfinder' maps cover the route in case you choose to buy them.

As the OS map is so good, why would you need this book as well? There are quite a few reasons why a guidebook based on knowledge of the district will help you. Firstly, although the map shows rights of way it does not distinguish between the ones which are easy walking and those which are muddy, overgrown or obstructed. Secondly there is the 'white road' problem; one of the few weaknesses of OS maps is that a pair of parallel lines, solid or broken, with white between them may be a public road, a private drive or farm track, or occasionally even a stream bed. Sometimes you can tell that a 'white road' is public because rights of way end on it, but this doesn't always help. Thirdly there are some paths which are not rights of way but where there is formal or informal acceptance of public use – only a few recognised 'concessionary paths' appear on the map. Fourthly, apart from formal car parks the map does not show where it is safe (and acceptable) to park. And lastly the map does not tell you which paths are attractive and which are boring, although the skilled map reader will find some clues. (Incidentally, for the benefit of a certain reviewer, writing a footpath guide involves much more than just looking at the map; it takes far more effort, for less reward, than the youngest of newspaper reporters would put up with).

The one-inch to the mile Ordnance Survey 'Peak District touring map and guide' is also an excellent map, and I recommend it for finding your way to the start of these walks. It is layer-contoured, so gives a better idea of the lie of the land to those who are not at home with contour lines. It shows footpaths (though those whose eyesight is less than perfect will find them hard to see), but I cannot recommend it as a footpath map because it does not show field boundaries, and it is often vital that you know which side of a fence to look for the path. However, the directions in this book should solve that sort of problem for you, so the one-inch map is an adequate companion. If you are familiar with the red-covered 1:50000 'Landranger' OS maps, note that the one-inch map is on a slightly smaller scale. Incidentally, on my copy of this map the emphasised grid lines are not at the usual '0' and '5' points; if yours is the same, don't get caught out.

Paths and stiles

The walks described follow rights of way or recognised concessionary footpaths, with a very few exceptions. On these few I found the paths clear, well-used and unobstructed. I cannot promise that they will be available to you, but I should be surprised if they were not. The descriptions of the walks make it clear which paths these are. Concessionary footpaths may of course be closed, although this is most unusual. Rights of way should be unobstructed and I have found them so as far as the walks in this book are concerned. If you do find an obstruction, you will do future walkers a service if you report it to any Peak Park information office, or to the Ramblers Association who will know what action to take. Remember that muddy patches and animals are not legally an obstruction, not even bulls if these are with dairy herds – all these animals are harmless. Farm dogs (and occasionally geese) can be alarming, but even so I have never been attacked by one; they are normally trained to know where the public is tolerated, and will do no more than bark if you keep to the path and show by your behaviour that you are confident of your right to be there.

Those who are new to this part of the country should note that a Peak District stile is not usually the wooden rail-and-plank structure of more southerly counties, although there are some of these. It is more likely to be a narrow gap, flanked by large stones, in a stone wall (a 'squeezer stile'), or stone steps built into each side of the wall ('step stile') – these can be difficult to spot from a distance; or sometimes a wooden ladder leading over the wall ('ladder stile'). When there is no stile but only a gate, open this rather than climbing it if possible. On a 'bridle path' the gate should definitely be able to be opened; on a 'footpath' you may have to climb. There is a wide variety of fastenings, ranging from a loop of string or even barbed wire to metal fasteners of Chinese Puzzle standard, but a little ingenuity will deal with most of them. You will often need to lift the catch end of the gate to open it even when the catch is undone. Remember to leave the gate fastened if you found it so.

Most but not all footpaths are signposted where they leave a public road, which may be just a track rather than a metalled road, and you will sometimes find signposts elsewhere.

Squeezer stile at Alstonefield

The most popular paths are waymarked with small yellow arrows or just blobs of yellow paint (sometimes light blue for a bridleway); this will be done especially if a footpath has been diverted to a new route, for example to avoid a farmyard. But many paths are not marked in any way, so you must depend on a guidebook like this or a 2½ inch map. If in doubt about the right way through a farm, ask anyone who is in sight; the farmer will appreciate your asking rather than pressing on, and will probably be glad to pass the time of day with you. But don't argue about rights of way with a farmer; route changes may take some time to appear on maps, and in any case you can't win even if he is wrong!

Transport

Most walkers reach their starting point by car these days, and I have indicated safe parking places at the start of each walk – sometimes a choice, for the benefit of people coming to the area from different directions. (I mean safe from a traffic point of view; unfortunately thieves have been known to visit the more rural car parks, so lock your car and do not leave anything tempting in sight). Do take care not to park where you may obstruct the road or a farm gate, however little it looks to be used – don't park in what looks like a lay-by opposite a farm gate either, the farmer may need the space to swing round with a large trailer. And of course, don't park in passing places on narrow roads. Open grassland alongside an unfenced road usually counts as farm land rather than part of the road, and parking will not be welcomed by the farmer. If you follow the directions in this book you should not have this sort of problem.

Public transport is scarce in this part of the Park. There are some bus services, though these are mostly timed for the convenience of residents and schoolchildren rather than walkers. Where I believe that a bus service may be useful, I have mentioned it. In particular you may find a use for the special ramblers' services which run on summer weekends. I have not given bus timetables, because many services change from time to time. Derbyshire County Council publish a complete timetable of all bus and train services in the Peak District (including those outside Derbyshire itself) twice a year, with updates in between. This is obtainable from Peak Park information centres and from the Public Transport Unit, Derbyshire County Council, Chatsworth Hall, Chesterfield Road, Matlock DE4 3FW; at the time of writing it costs £1 including postage. It is essential reading for those without their own transport, and also useful if you want to plan a walk that does not return to its starting point. For individual services you can enquire by telephone; ring Busline on Buxton (01298) 23098.

No railways remain in the part of the National Park covered by this book, but there is a regular (if not always punctual) service to Buxton from Manchester and beyond. This is included in the timetable mentioned above.

Eating

Any of these walks can be completed in half a day, and we have often found it convenient to take a morning walk and then find lunch at a quiet pub. One of the happiest developments of the last couple of decades has been the spread of lunchtime catering to country pubs, especially in areas like the Peak. So I have mentioned suitable pubs near to each walk. Most of them we have visited and enjoyed; a few of those mentioned I have not visited, but I know from other sources that food is available. At all the pubs I mention there is lunchtime food both at weekends and during the week, but a few publicans have a day off during the week, so be prepared to try elsewhere if necessary. I have not generally looked for pubs actually on the route of the walk, partly for this reason and partly because muddy boots are not always welcome – though one couple I saw recently had solved this problem by putting tough plastic bags over their boots as they entered. Children are welcome at most pubs at lunchtime nowadays, if not always in the evening. There are a few cafes in this area, but nowadays the sign 'Farmhouse teas' has become rare – no doubt something to do with EC food hygiene regulations.

Remember that landlords and cooks change from time to time. I cannot promise that your lunch will be as good as mine was, nor that the attitude to children will be the same. If you are disappointed by the meal (or if you particularly enjoy it), tell the landlord and not me! On the other hand, if you find that a pub has given up serving lunchtime food or excludes children, I should like to hear of it (via the publisher) so that I can correct any future edition.

I am no connoisseur of ale, so this is not a 'Pub walks' guide in the sense of the series published by Sigma. I enjoy a drink to help my lunch down, but on the whole I judge a pub by its ability to serve good simple hot food, reasonably promptly, in a friendly (and not too smoky) atmosphere. A few country pubs have moved up-market, and turned themselves into fashionable restaurants. Good luck to them; but this is not the sort of pub I look for when I am out walking.

Safety and Courtesy

There are many abandoned mineshafts in the Peak District. Most of them have been made safe, but a few have not. Don't let your children get too near, because the ground may crumble. A conical depression may be a run-in mineshaft; again, most are safe, but it's better not to take a risk. You may find horizontal mine tunnels ('adits' or 'levels') or natural caves that are open too. Treat these with caution; if you must venture in, don't go further than you can see. Remember that there may be shafts in the floor of the tunnel, sometimes hidden by rotten wood, or boulders dangerously balanced above you. Better to take your children to one of the mines or caves that are open to the public – for example at Castleton, Buxton or Matlock Bath.

I have not taken a dog on any of these walks. If you do, please make sure that it is on a lead whenever there are other animals in sight – they may be harmed if scared by the sight of even the most placid dog.

I feel tempted to say the same about very small children; not to the extent of putting them on a lead, of course, but for their own safety do make sure that they are close to you when there are animals about. Take especial care near crags and rivers. Teach your children to watch out for barbed wire, and don't let them climb on walls, fences or gates: they may well hurt themselves and they will certainly not please the farmer. Occasionally a gate on a public footpath is padlocked or otherwise fixed, and you will have to climb over. Make sure your children know that they should climb at the hinge end of the gate.

And finally, follow the countryside code, which is really just common sense – don't disturb animals, don't trample crops, don't start fires, leave gates as you find them (unless a gate is open which should obviously be shut, for example to keep animals off the road), don't damage walls or fences or obstruct lanes or gateways, and in particular remember that the countryside is the farmer's livelihood as well as his home. With very few exceptions, country people are friendly people; but one thoughtless walker can queer the pitch for the many that follow.

Enjoy your walking!

Postscript

The toilet block at the Derbyshire Bridge car park, mentioned in several walks, has recently been destroyed by fire. Until it is rebuilt the nearest alternatives are in Buxton, either just past the traffic lights on the A54 near Burbage church or at the Grin Low car park (SK047721). There are also toilets at Goytsclough Quarry, closed in winter, but these cannot be reached from Derbyshire Bridge because the road is one-way.

Walk 1: Lyme Park

Start: park on an open patch on the verge of the minor road which leads southwards from Higher Disley to join the B5470 Whaley Bridge to Macclesfield road, just north of the disused drive to the East Lodge of Lyme Park (SJ982832). There is room for several cars.

You can also use the car park close to Lyme Hall (SJ963823: enter the park from the A6 at Park Gate near Disley); but there is a substantial fee for cars entering the park, except for National Trust members. If you park here, walk up the hill, passing left of the house and stable block, and turn right through a gate just beyond the stables; you are now on the main route.

Distance: 3½ miles (alternatives 3 to 4½ miles).

Map: this walk is outside the area covered by the Ordnance Survey 'Outdoor Leisure' 1:25000 maps, though it is covered by the OS 1 inch to the mile 'Peak District Touring Map'. If you want a larger scale map it will be the OS Pathfinder (1:25000) sheet 741 (SJ88/98) 'Stockport (South)'.

Public transport: there are several bus routes along the A6 which stop at the park gate, 200 yards from the route of this walk. They include a service between Buxton and Stockport at least every half hour, and less frequent buses to Derby and Nottingham. Disley station, on the Manchester to Buxton line, is about half a mile from the route of the walk.

Lyme Park occupies the northern tip of the section of the Peak Park that is covered by this book. The park and the house at its centre, Lyme Hall, were once the seat of the Legh family but are now owned by the National Trust, and most of the 1300 acres of the park are open freely to pedestrians during daylight hours. The house and gardens are also open, with an admission charge, at certain times.

Much of Lyme Park is conventional parkland, with well-spaced trees, and woodland; but the eastern part is open moor rising to 1200 feet. The park is home to a large and long-established herd of deer, which can usually be found in the eastern part of the park away from the throng of visitors, and also a small herd of Highland cattle.

This walk is partly within Lyme Park and partly down the Bollinhurst Valley just outside it. It is entirely within Cheshire; most of the walk is

Lyme Park

within the Peak Park, though that part which is outside the Lyme Park boundary is outside the Peak Park too. There is no road walking. The walk is on gritstone; most of it is suitable for all weathers, though there may be a few muddy patches. The park is hilly and there are some quite steep ascents.

The Walk

Walk a few yards south along the road and turn right into the disused drive towards East Lodge. In 200 yards this is crossed by a footpath; go right over the stile and ahead towards a stream but not across it, and then bear left down the left side of a wooded valley. A faint track brings you to a wall (the enclosure of Bollinhurst reservoir) and bears right alongside it to Cockhead Farm. Go straight through the farmyard, through an iron gate, and on across the field (with Horse Coppice reservoir well to your left) to a gate and stile on the left of a little valley. Beyond the stile the path is enclosed by fences, and soon meets a tarmac drive; turn right along this. Lyme Park is now just over the wall on your left. In a few hundred yards you will come to an imposing gate beside a lodge; go through it and down the track to join the tarmac access road by the ticket-seller's hut (no charge for pedestrians).

1. LYME PARK

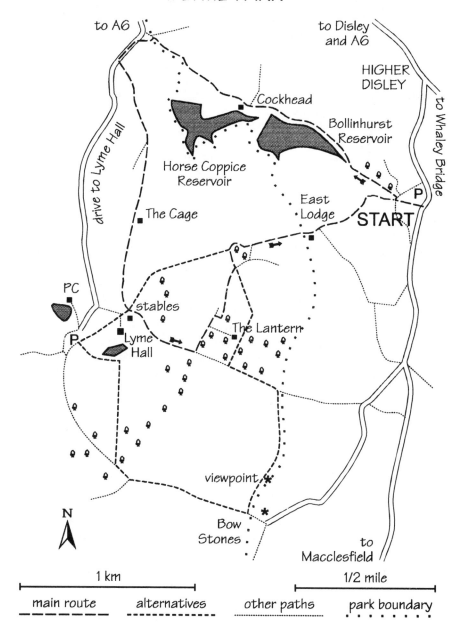

to A6

to Disley
and A6

HIGHER
DISLEY

to Whaley Bridge

Cockhead

Bollinhurst
Reservoir

drive to Lyme Hall

Horse Coppice
Reservoir

The Cage

East
Lodge

P

START

PC

P

stables

The Lantern

Lyme
Hall

viewpoint

N

Bow
Stones

to
Macclesfield

1 km	1/2 mile

| main route | alternatives | other paths | park boundary |

Turn left over a little bridge, and in a few yards (at the end of the embankment) fork left off the tarmac road onto a rough track which runs up the ridge. Where this track bears right, keep straight ahead over the grass of the ridge to Lyme Cage, a turreted tower which has been in sight for most of the walk. It was built in the 16th century as a viewpoint, perhaps for watching the progress of the hunt, and remodelled in the 18th century. There is now no access to the interior, but it is certainly worth admiring the view from its foot; in one direction the whole Manchester conurbation, with Alderley Edge to its left; in the other the Pennine moors stretching to Kinder Scout.

Continue along the ridge until Lyme Hall comes in sight straight ahead of you, with the imposing stable block to its left. Go through an iron gate (marked 'No cycling)' to the left of the stables, and follow a firm track which passes the gardens on the right and then a small wood. You will come to a very tall ladder stile with a wooden gate beside it, but do not cross it; instead turn left along a green track, parallel with the bottom of Lantern Wood. Shortly you will see, in a clearing in the wood, the Lantern. This is an ornamental feature made of Elizabethan masonry discarded when the hall was rebuilt in 1725. You can cross a stile to visit it if you wish.

A sign directs pedestrians to the right, alongside a cross wall, and over a stile into the wood. Turn left just inside the wood and you will soon come to a step-stile in a stone wall which leads you onto open moorland. Follow the path, roughly parallel with a wall but separated from it by a patch of rushes, until you see a small isolated wood on your left, and fork towards it (the path ahead becomes very muddy). There is a stile in the fence on each side of the wood; cross either, and turn right along the drive. This leads to East Lodge, where there is a gate in the high wall that keeps the deer within the park. Go through the gate and follow the disused drive for half a mile back to the road; your starting point is a few yards to the left.

Alternatives

For a shorter walk, do not go through the gate to the left of the stables but turn left along the drive, which is metalled at first and later gravel. Follow it to East Lodge; the main route joins the drive before you reach the lodge.

For an extra mile, do not turn left at the stables but continue down the hill past the Hall to the car park. Follow the wall at the left of the car park to a stile marked 'Nature trail and Moorland trail'. Go over the stile, up the broad steps and alongside the garden fence, with a fine view of the south front of Lyme Hall across the lake. When you reach a gate ahead of you, do not go through but turn right (as waymarked for the trails) along an avenue of trees. This climbs to the edge of a wood. Go through the gate and straight on up the track into the wood for a hundred yards until you meet a cross track. Turn left along it. You are now on the route of the Gritstone Trail, a long-distance footpath which starts at the Lyme Hall car park and ends in the Dane Valley, east of Congleton, where it joins the Staffordshire Way.

The track leaves the wood at a gate and stile and bears slightly left to climb the moor, aiming just right of a group of radio aerials on the skyline, to reach the park wall at Bowstonegate. Do not pass through the gate but turn left alongside the wall (if you wish you can make a short diversion out of the park to see the Bow Stones, a pair of Saxon cross shafts now very much eroded; they are close to the farmhouse gate).

Follow the ridge, keeping alongside the wall and passing a viewpoint with a direction indicator. Where this wall meets another, turn left alongside it. Ignore a step stile in the wall, but cross a ladder stile over the wall into the wood, and follow a path straight ahead – faint at first, but later marked by log kerbs. Passing the Lantern on your left, continue till you leave the wood at another stile. Bear rather to the left along a visible path, aiming for a small isolated wood. Go over the stile either side of it and turn right along the gravel drive to East Lodge: you are now back on the main route.

After heavy rain the path by the reservoirs may be rather wet. You can avoid this by walking right down the drive, past East Lodge, to the Hall and then continuing by the route suggested as the longer alternative above.

Amenities

There are public toilets and a cafeteria in the park, at a group of buildings by the lake in the valley bottom below Lyme Hall. (These arrangements may change now that the National Trust has taken over the park management from the local authority).

There is a refreshment kiosk at the main car park near to the Hall, and several pubs in Disley. If you turn the other way from your starting point and continue towards Macclesfield, you will come to the Highwayman Inn in about four miles, and the Robin Hood (a favourite of mine) in another mile.

Walk 2: Taxal and Windgather

Start: the walk starts, for convenience of parking, at the large layby (a bend cut off by road improvements) on the west side of the A5004 Buxton to Whaley Bridge road where the track from Shallcross Hall to Taxal crosses it (SK009799). This is half a mile south of the traffic lights at the south end of Whaley Bridge (Horwich End), and a mile south of Whaley Bridge station. The only safe parking in Taxal village is in the church car park, which you may be able to use on a weekday. It is difficult to park on the other minor roads on the route.

Distance: 4 miles (alternatives 3½ to 5½ miles).

Public transport: Whaley Bridge station has an hourly service (not always punctual) on the Manchester – Stockport – Buxton line. There are occasional buses from here to Fernilee, passing the starting point. Several bus services pass the Horwich End traffic lights half a mile from the starting point, including a half-hourly service (hourly on Sundays) between Buxton and Stockport and a two-hourly Nottingham – Derby – Buxton – Manchester service; these run to Buxton via Chapel-en-le-Frith, not by the direct route past Fernilee. From the traffic lights walk up the A5004 towards Buxton for a quarter of a mile (there is a footway) and then take a track on the right, opposite Mevril Road; when you reach a cross path, turn right over the footbridge to Taxal.

This walk takes you from the tiny village of Taxal up onto Taxal Moor and to Windgather Rocks, a rocky cliff popular with climbers, on Taxal Edge. It then drops to the Goyt valley below Fernilee and runs through farmland back to the starting point.

The walk is mainly in Derbyshire, but crosses the Cheshire boundary where it runs along the top of the ridge. It is entirely on gritstone. It is manageable after rain, though parts of the moor will be soggy. About a mile is along quiet byroads. The starting point is just outside the Peak Park boundary, but all but a few yards of the walk are within the Park.

The starting point and a few hundred yards of this walk are the same as for walk 3, and the two can be combined to give a walk of about 5½ miles.

2. TAXAL AND WINDGATHER

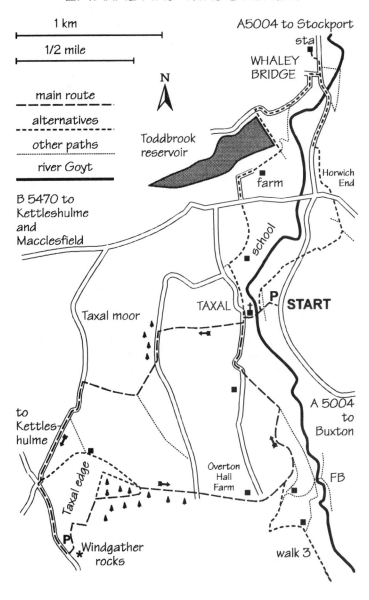

The Walk

From the centre of the layby, turn down the steep walled track which crosses the river and climbs to the picturesque church at Taxal. Turn left along the road for a few yards, past the rectory gate, and then go right over a step stile by an iron gate (footpath sign). Go straight up the hillside through several fields, till you meet a metalled road. Turn left along it for a hundred yards, then at the end of a wood take an obvious track slanting right up the hillside, and then bearing right to cross the ridge of Taxal Moor.

Continue to the road and turn left. At the crossroads in a quarter of a mile turn left. In rather over a quarter of a mile you will come to a layby, where there is a signposted path on the left leading in a very short distance to Windgather rocks. Gain the top of the rocks and turn left above the cliff until the path turns right, then left and right again, through a corner of the wood. (If you miss this path you can follow the edge of the wood to its corner and turn right down the side of the wood).

Follow the path straight down the slope, with the wood a short way to your right. The path crosses a tarmac byroad about 50 yards from where the road ends at the edge of the wood, and continues to the right of the wall to pass to the right of Overton Hall Farm where it becomes a track. About 200 yards beyond the farm, the metalled track turns very sharp right; go straight ahead along a green trackway. Where this ends at a gateway, bear left along a faint green path parallel to the top of the wood. The path bends to the right as it dips into a side valley, where you cross a tiny stream. Beyond the stile, follow the clear green path diagonally across the field to a pair of isolated stone gateposts, and onwards aiming just right of an isolated house. Join the road at a footpath sign and turn right along it. In a quarter of a mile you will be back at Taxal church; turn right just before it to return to your starting point.

Alternative routes

You can save half a mile, at the cost of missing Windgather rocks, if you turn left into a farm road when you have walked a quarter mile along the road you joined after going over Taxal Moor – this is a few yards before the crossroads. Turn right past the farm, and you will rejoin the main route where it runs down the hill alongside the wood towards Overton Hall Farm.

By linking this walk with Walk 3, which takes you to the Fernilee dam, you can extend it to about 5½ miles. Pass Overton Hall Farm as described, but turn sharp right in 200 yards with the metalled track. Beyond the gate of Madscar farm the track becomes rougher. It turns sharp left as it crosses Mill Clough, passes behind Knipe Farm, and bends right to run straight to the Fernilee dam. You are now on the route of walk 3, and you should follow the instructions there to return to your starting point.

If you start the walk at Whaley Bridge station you can avoid walking along the main road through the town, at the expense of an extra quarter mile or so. Turn under the railway bridge by the station, away from the main road, and go straight ahead (ignoring the road on the right which passes the back entrance of the station) along a quiet residential road which leads to the Toddbrook reservoir. This reservoir supplies water to the Peak Forest canal, which starts below the station at Whaley Bridge.

When you reach the reservoir, turn left across the dam and then go through a stile on the right (waymarked 'Midshires Way') and walk along a clear path through the field, with the hedge on your left and the reservoir on the right. A stile brings you to Reddish Farm; go to the right of the farmhouse and follow the farm road, with new houses on your left, till it reaches the main road. Go straight across, through a stile, and follow the clear path across fields to an iron gate. Do not go through it but follow the fence to the right of it up the field, as waymarked. (This patch may be wet – if so, backtrack a bit and go to the right of the wet patch). The path continues across a drive and through a wood (in wet weather, it may be best to go a few yards right up the drive to the road, and then left along it), and brings you out on the road just before Taxal church; turn left, and your stile is on the right just beyond the rectory.

At the end of the walk you can take another way back from Taxal to Whaley Bridge station. Turn down by the church and cross the river, then take the track through the gate on the left. (If you are coming from the Walk 3 route, go straight across the lane from the layby to Taxal; the path runs parallel to the track from the gate, and joins it at a stile). At the main road go straight across and up Mevril Road opposite. Just before this ends there is a recreation ground on the right. Turn into this and go down the fenced path behind the goalposts, at the end of the mesh fence. This path takes you over a footbridge and then between two factories to a minor road. Turn left, between new houses, and then right along a broad gravel path beyond the last house. This is the route of the old Cromford and High Peak railway, of which you will see more on walk 3; the factories occupy part of the old goods yard.

Go on under the road. The broad path ends abruptly, where a bridge under the present railway is blocked, but an alley on the left takes you to the main road. Turn right along it, past the Cock Inn (food) and under the railway. You will reach the station in a quarter of a mile. However, if you want to see a bit more of the Cromford and High Peak route, turn sharply right up Old Road just before you reach the river bridge (or take a short cut up the path past the Shepherds Arms). In a hundred yards turn sharp left onto the railway route, which again is a broad gravel path. Shortly it turns and slopes downhill; this is the Whaley Incline, the shortest of all the inclines on the CHPR and unusual in that for much of its life it was worked by a horse-powered windlass rather than a steam engine. The short section of line from the goods yard you passed to the canal remained in use until 1952.

At the bottom of the slope your route is left, up Bridge Street, to the station; but if time permits, go on over the iron bridge (with the rails still in place) to see the canal terminus, now a hire boat base. The CHPR railway line ran in through each of the side arches, while the centre arch was for boats.

Taxal Church

Amenities

There is no longer an inn in Taxal village. If you turn right out of the car park you will come to the Shady Oak inn at Fernilee in a mile; you can continue to Buxton, where there are many inns and cafes, if you wish. If you turn left into Whaley Bridge there are cafes, a fish and chip shop, and several inns which serve food at lunchtime.

There are no public toilets on the route of this walk; the nearest are at Whaley Bridge, on the main road near the station, or in Buxton.

Walk 3: Taxal and Fernilee

Start: at the large layby on the west side of the A5004 Buxton to Whaley Bridge road (SK009799), half a mile south of the traffic lights at the south end of Whaley Bridge (Horwich End) and a mile south of Whaley Bridge station.

Alternatively, park at the Fernilee dam (SK015777). This is reached by a rough tarmac road, signed 'Goyt Water Treatment Works', which leaves the A5004 about half a mile north of the Shady Oak inn at Fernilee.

Distance: 3 miles (alternatives 2 to 5½ miles).

Public transport: see Walk 2.

The starting point and a few hundred yards of the walk are the same as for walk 2. The two can be combined to make a 5½ mile walk; see the walk 2 directions.

This walk takes you up a wooded section of the Goyt Valley from Taxal to the dam of Fernilee reservoir, with an optional extension round the reservoir. It returns down the other side of the river and through Shallcross wood. It is entirely in Derbyshire. It should be reasonable in most weather conditions; there will be some muddy patches after rain, which can be avoided by the routes suggested under 'Alternatives'. The walk is best in the spring, when the leaves are just beginning to open in the woods.

The Walk

Take the walled track which leads down from the middle of the layby, cross the footbridge over the river Goyt, and climb to the road at Taxal church. This has an interesting tower; the rest is Victorian. Turn left along the road. Ignore a footpath on the right (the route of walk 2).

The road dips to cross a stream. In 50 yards, at a footpath signpost, fork left along a faint green path and aim for the right-hand end of a walled wood. (If the first part of the field is muddy, stay on the road as far as a house gate before cutting across to the path). At an isolated pair of stone gateposts the path forks. Take the left fork and cross a wooden stile into Hillbridge wood, by a sign telling you that this is a nature

3. TAXAL AND FERNILEE

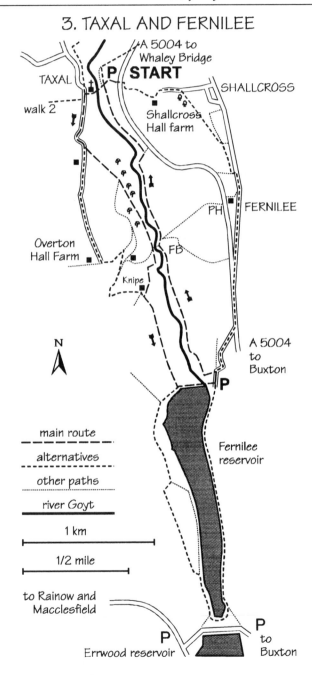

reserve. It has bluebells, violets and wood anemones in May. The path runs through the wood, dropping gently towards the river.

Just beyond a bench seat you will find a wooden stile and a footbridge over the Goyt. Cross the stile, but not the bridge; instead go over a wooden stile in a wire fence on your right, then bear left and cross a little bridge over a side stream. A footpath leads up the slope, parallel to an old sunken track, past a waymark post marked 'Knipe'.

Beyond a wooden gate the path is enclosed and muddy for a short way until it crosses a wooden stile into a field. Go straight on, past a tree, aiming to the left of a house. Do not go through the gate marked 'Knipe farm', but go further left between a tree and an electricity pole and then through a narrow wooden gate in the wall. Bear left alongside the wall to reach a farm road and turn left along it. In half a mile you will reach the dam of the Fernilee reservoir, built in the 1930s to meet Stockport's water supply needs.

Cross the dam and turn left, passing the parking space. At a cross-roads, where the tarmac road turns right, notice the level track ahead (marked 'No Entry') but do not take it – it is not a right of way, and is obstructed at the next farm. This track and the one alongside the reservoir behind you are the course of the Cromford and High Peak railway, opened in 1831 to link the Cromford canal, in the Derwent valley near Matlock, with the Peak Forest canal at Whaley Bridge. This section was closed in 1892 when it was superseded by the Ashbourne – Buxton – Whaley bridge line. The CHPR was designed as a series of level stretches, like this, which were originally worked by horses and later by steam locomotives. They were linked by steep inclines where the trucks were raised and lowered on cables by a stationary steam engine – you can see one of these engines preserved at Middleton Top near Wirksworth. Another incline is now used by the road from Buxton to the Errwood reservoir, and a third is met on one of the alternative routes to Walk 2.

Turn left at this junction, onto the metalled road which winds down the hillside below the dam. Beyond the water treatment works this continues as a gravel track, and then a green footpath. After the second stile you will come to the other end of the footbridge you passed on the outward journey. Do not cross it, but continue alongside the river through two fields and into Shallcross wood. Eventually you will come out on the walled track that leads across the Goyt to Taxal. Turn right along it to return to your starting point.

Fernilee Reservoir

Alternative routes

For a much shorter walk (under two miles), cross the footbridge when you reach it and turn left.

In wet weather the path through Hillbridge Wood and up to Knipe may be muddy. You can avoid this by staying on the metalled road from Taxal church until it ends at Overton Hall Farm. Now turn left down a firm farm track, and in 200 yards turn sharp right. Stay on this track, which turns sharp left as it crosses a side valley; it passes above Knipe Farm, and the main route to the reservoir rejoins it just beyond.

An alternative way from the Fernilee dam back to your starting point, which adds less than half a mile, is by way of Fernilee village and Shallcross Hall Farm. This avoids Shallcross Wood, which may be muddy after rain. From the dam, follow the tarmac access road uphill to the main road, and turn left along it – there is a footway. Fork right up a byroad in about 200 yards (if you stay on the main road you will reach the Shady Oak Inn in a quarter of a mile, and can regain the byroad by a lane just beyond the inn). You will pass an old chapel and come to a group of cottages. Immediately beyond the last of these, go through an iron wicket gate on the left, where the cottage entry joins the road, and turn left alongside the hedge. Very soon another gate brings you onto a green walled track. Turn right along it.

This is another section of the old Cromford and High Peak railway; this section is obviously used by walkers, although it is not a right of way and does not form a through route. In about 200 yards there is a blocked gate facing you on the left; cross the stile in the wall a few yards beyond it. (You could reach this point by staying on the lane, then going through a very inconspicuous stile on the left just beyond a cross wall, opposite a large farm). Turn half-right across the field, making for a row of big trees at the top of the rise. Follow the trees to the road, where you will find a stile in the wooden fence a few yards to the right of the field corner. Turn left, past Shallcross Hall Farm; the road becomes a track, and descends to the main road opposite the layby where the walk started.

Extending the walk round Fernilee reservoir will add 2½ miles. When you reach the dam, do not cross it but take the track which leads to the right of the reservoir. Where the track turns sharp right, leave it by a stile half hidden by bushes, signposted 'Errwood Dam'. In half a mile, as you come to a side valley, the way forks; you can take either as they rejoin later. At the head of the reservoir, walk round the end and join the firm level path that leads along the other side. This is the track of the old railway. When you reach the other end of the Fernilee dam you are back on the main route.

Amenities

There is no longer an inn in Taxal village. If you turn right out of the car park you will come to the Shady Oak inn at Fernilee in a mile; you can continue to Buxton, where there are many inns and cafes, if you wish. If you turn left there are inns, cafes and a chip shop in Whaley Bridge.

There are no public toilets on the route of this walk; the nearest are at Whaley Bridge, on the main road near the station, or in Buxton. If you take the extension round Fernilee reservoir you will find a public toilet at the Bunsal Cob car park, a short way to the east of the Errwood dam, but this may be closed in winter.

Walk 4: Goyt Valley and White Hall

Start: at the Bunsal Cob car park (SK019759) just east of the dam of Errwood reservoir, four miles south of Whaley Bridge. The car park is usually fairly quiet; there is a larger, busier car park (and sometimes an ice cream van) just beyond the reservoir dam (SK013757).

Note that you cannot enter the Goyt Valley from the south, near the junction of the A54 and A537 roads west of Buxton: the road between the Derbyshire Bridge car park and the Errwood reservoir is open only to southbound traffic, and is closed entirely on summer Sundays.

There is car parking space near the dam of the lower (Fernilee) reservoir (SK015777), down the waterworks road. It is difficult to park on the minor road near White Hall.

Distance: 4½ miles (alternatives 4½ to 6½ miles).

Public transport: there are a very few buses from Whaley Bridge station to Fernilee village on four days a week, but none between there and Buxton.

The route should be avoided after very rainy weather as the first section will have wet patches.

This walk climbs from the Goyt valley to the ridge at White Hall, follows a very minor road for a mile and descends across the fields to Fernilee village. It then passes the dam of Fernilee reservoir and continues alongside the water, on the route of the old Cromford and High Peak railway, to return to the starting point.

This walk is entirely in Derbyshire, on gritstone. A hundred yards or so is along a main road, which has a footway. Another mile is along a very quiet byroad.

The Walk

At the bottom end of the Bunsal Cob car park, a footpath sign on the right points to a stile. Cross this and follow the path to the right, down through the trees. After a slight rise it drops again to a stile and footbridge. Cross these and take the path which zigzags steeply up the hillside; when you pause for breath, turn and admire the view of the

4. GOYT VALLEY AND WHITE HALL

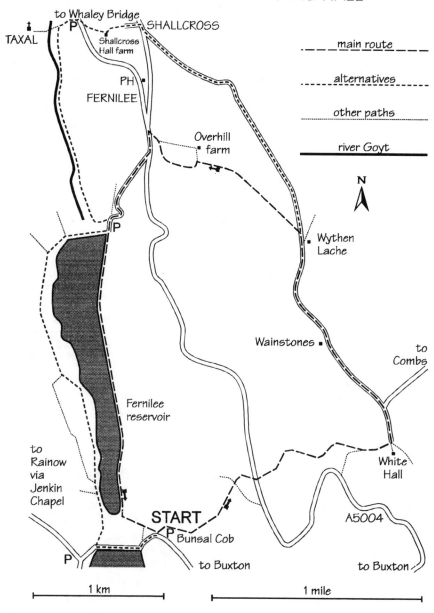

to Whaley Bridge

SHALLCROSS

TAXAL

Shallcross
Hall farm

PH
FERNILEE

Overhill
farm

P

Wythen
Lache

Wainstones

to
Combs

Fernilee
reservoir

to
Rainow
via
Jenkin
Chapel

White
Hall

START
P Bunsal Cob

A5004

P

to Buxton

to Buxton

— · — main route — · —

— — — · — — — alternatives — — — · — — —

············ other paths ············

━━━━━ river Goyt

N

1 km

1 mile

reservoir. Beyond a gate and stile the path becomes a track. Follow this path past a couple of footpath signs pointing back the way you came, ignoring cross paths, till it eventually turns right and comes to the main A5004 road.

Go straight across the road and through the gate opposite, and take the obvious path bearing left up the hillside. Towards the top it bends to the right, then left through a gap in the wall. The buildings of White Hall (a Derbyshire County Council outdoor pursuits centre) can be seen in trees straight ahead. To the right you can see the main road winding up the hill, and below it an earlier but steeper route, the first turnpike from Buxton to Whaley bridge.

The footpath joins a walled track at a gate a short way from the hall. Turn left along this, and at the hall gate turn left along the tarmac road. Follow this for about a mile, bearing left at the fork, down a dip and over a ridge. Here you have a distant view of Kinder Scout, the peaty plateau which is the highest part of the Peak District. Continue past Wythen Lache farm, ignoring the track which forks right. Shortly after this, just before the road passes through a gateway, cross a steep stile on the left which has a wooden handrail.

Take the path which bears right across a large field. Beyond a marshy patch the path becomes indistinct; carry on in the same direction, or slightly more to the right, until two farmhouses come in sight, and aim for those. An obvious gate will be seen where the wall joins a fence, but aim for a less conspicuous gate a little to the left, identified by a sign saying 'stile'.

Beyond this gate follow a track alongside the wall down to the farm road. The official right of way leads to the right almost to Overhill farm and then down a field to rejoin the farm road, but the farmer would doubtless prefer you to turn left and follow the farm road down; this is drier and shorter. Turn right where the farm road runs into another lane and you will soon reach the main road.

Turn left along the road (which has a footway) for about 100 yards and fork right down the waterworks drive. This brings you to the dam of Fernilee reservoir; the water treatment works is hidden by trees in the valley below. Don't cross the dam, but turn left and follow the roadway alongside the reservoir. This was originally the track of the Cromford and High Peak railway, of which more is said in the description of walks 2 and 3. Walk the length of the reservoir, to the Errwood reservoir dam, and go up the slope on your left to the starting point. You may notice, as you approach the car park, that the railway turns and climbs through the trees below it to join the track you have just walked;

it has been partly filled in to make the car park, but you can see it emerging from a bridge below the car park fence. Above the car park the railway incline is now used by the road to Buxton.

Alternative routes

You can take a slightly longer, but muddier, route around the far side of Fernilee reservoir. After coming down the waterworks drive, cross the dam and bear left with the reservoir on your left. Where the track turns right, cross a stile on the left almost hidden by bushes. The path runs through the trees for the length of the reservoir, and ends on the road near the Errwood dam. Cross the dam and continue for 200 yards to your starting point.

For a walk which is about two miles longer, go to White Hall and take the tarmac road as far as Wythen Lache as described, but instead of going over the stile continue along the road. In a mile and a half you will come to the Shallcross estate. Turn left near the telephone box (which is almost hidden in the hedge on your left), onto a road which becomes a lane passing Shallcross Hall farm. Cross the main road and take a track almost opposite, at the middle of the layby, which leads across the Goyt towards Taxal, but before reaching the river take a path on the left. This leads through the riverside meadows to the Fernilee dam, where you rejoin the main route.

Amenities

Return from the car park to the Buxton to Whaley Bridge road. If you turn left you can eat at the Shady Oak in Fernilee, three miles down the road. Or turn right for a wide choice of inns and cafes in Buxton.

The pleasant drive along the narrow one-way road up the Goyt Valley will eventually bring you to the Cat and Fiddle on the Buxton to Macclesfield road; if you pass this and fork left you will come to the Stanley Arms at the head of Wildboarclough. On the right near this fork you will find a cafe. This road up the Goyt valley is closed to all traffic on summer Sundays.

There are public toilets at the car park where the walk starts, but these may be closed in winter. In this case the nearest will be at Derbyshire Bridge, three miles up the Goyt Valley (you will pass toilets at Goyts Clough quarry on the way, but these will probably be closed too), or in Buxton.

Walk 5: Buxton to Chapel-en-le-Frith station

Start: Buxton station, or a nearby parking place. There are car parks near the station, but it is easier to park in the quiet 'Park' residential area which is just to the left of the A5004 Whaley Bridge road; turn opposite the large domed building (the Devonshire hospital). This turning leads to a road which goes round in a circle; turn right along it and park at the roadside. Then walk on to the next turning on the right, which brings you back up to the main road; turn left along it.

I have assumed that you will start from Buxton and return by train, but you can equally well park at Chapel-en-le-Frith station (a mile out of the town, grid reference SK055795) or approach from Manchester or beyond by train.

Distance: 4½ miles (alternative 5 miles).

Public transport: trains from Manchester and Stockport to Buxton via Chapel-en-le-Frith run hourly, weekdays and Sundays. Many of the trains come from further afield, and can be unpunctual. Chapel station is unstaffed; there is a slot machine for rail tickets, but you can also pay on the train.

There are buses to Buxton from several directions. There are also buses to Chapel-en-le-Frith but they run a good mile from the railway station; so if you wish to take a bus at the end of the journey, you can continue along the road through Combs Village and past the reservoir, and in a mile you will reach the B5470 main road. Here there are half-hourly buses (hourly on Sunday) between Buxton and Stockport, and a two-hourly service from Nottingham, Derby and Buxton to Stockport and Manchester.

Unlike the rest of the walks in the book, this does not bring you back to your starting point; instead it takes you to Chapel-en-le-Frith station from which there is an hourly rail service all day (weekdays and Sundays) back to Buxton. This has the minor advantage that there is more downhill than uphill – though the ups are fairly long and steep. The walk is entirely within Derbyshire, on gritstone. It starts and ends outside the Peak Park, although most of it is within the park. The first mile is alongside a main road (not a very busy one) but there is a footway for all but the last hundred yards, where there is an adequate grass verge.

Combs Edge

Most of the route is dry but there are one or two wet patches just beyond White Hall. These can be avoided, without increasing the distance, by walking along a quiet byroad for a mile and a half from White Hall to Combs village.

The Walk

From Buxton station go down the main road to the right, turn right at the roundabout, and fork right up the hill to pass left of the Devonshire Hospital with its huge dome. (Convenient parking is off to the left at the next turning after the Macclesfield road). Walk up the A5004 main road towards Whaley Bridge for a mile; this is a steep pull, but there is a good footway (grass verge for the last few yards) and the traffic is not heavy.

Where the main road swings sharply left, after the slope has eased, go straight ahead along a narrow tarmac lane. The tarmac ends by a disused reservoir but the lane goes on. It is in fact on the line of the old Roman road from Buxton to Glossop. At the road summit, where it becomes tarmac again, you enter the Peak Park. You are now at the highest point of the main route and you can avoid further uphill stretches if you wish. Carry on for another half mile, past a small wood on your left and a derelict pond on your right, till you reach another

5. BUXTON TO CHAPEL-EN-LE-FRITH

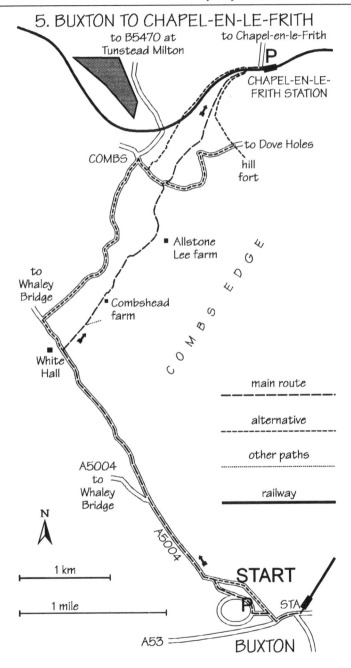

to B5470 at
Tunstead Milton

to Chapel-en-le-Frith

P

CHAPEL-EN-LE-
FRITH STATION

to Dove Holes

COMBS

hill
fort

Allstone
Lee farm

to
Whaley
Bridge

Combshead
farm

C O M B S   E D G E

White
Hall

main route

alternative

other paths

railway

A5004
to
Whaley
Bridge

N

1 km

1 mile

START

P

STA

BUXTON

A53

A5004

wood on your left which surrounds the White Hall Outdoor Pursuits Centre. Opposite the beginning of the wood, cross a stile on your right signposted 'Footpath to Combs and Chapel'. (If you prefer to take the by-road route to Combs, go on for another quarter of a mile along the road, passing White Hall, and turn right at a road junction. You will be in Combs village in about a mile and a quarter; turn left for the bus route, or right to continue the walk as described).

Keep the wall on your right and cross two muddy patches to a stile which faces you. Go over this and straight on, with the wall now on your left. Ignore a path which branches off shortly to your right (it leads to a shooting cabin on the edge of the moor and on along Combs Edge to the hill fort; but although unobstructed it is not a right of way, and the owner is not willing to make it a concessionary path). At the next gate, cross the stile and carry on with the fence and stream on your right, but keep at the top of the bank rather than down by the stream. Just to the left of all the buildings of Combshead farm, cross a farm track and a stile and go on to a gateway at a bend in the wall on your right. Through this, and keep left with the wall on your left until you see two gateways ahead. Take the right-hand one and continue with the wall on your left. Another stile takes you down to two streams, the first crossed by a wooden footbridge and the second by a stone slab. Bear rather to the right once you have crossed these, towards a gate; but instead of going through it, go just to the right and then up the field with the hedge (and an old sunken track, now a stream) on your left. At the top, with Allstone Lee farm on your right, you will be reassured by a footpath sign, footbridge and stile. Go ahead along the farm road, and you will drop to a road near Combs village.

If you've had enough hills, turn left along the road for 200 yards and then take the path by Old Brook House which leads under a railway bridge and then alongside the railway for a mile to Chapel-en-le-Frith station. Otherwise turn right along the road for a few yards and then left over a stile, which is also signposted to Chapel-en-le-Frith station. After a few yards of flagged path, go through a gateway and climb steeply up the field with the wall on your right. At the gateway on the skyline, pause for breath and admire the view over Coombs reservoir. Then continue on the level until you see a stile ahead, and cross it. Follow the path through a very long field and a patch of woodland until it descends to a drive. Turn left, under the railway bridge, then immediately right for the path to the station.

Alternative routes

If you have time to spare, you can visit the hill fort on Combs Edge after you reach the road at Combs village. The added distance is not great but it involves a climb of six or seven hundred feet.

When you reach the road near Combs, turn right along it but then continue along the road instead of crossing the stile on the left. The road climbs steeply, and at the crest there is a signpost and a stile on the right from which a clear path leads up to the ridge. If you then turn left along the edge, crossing a stile, you will find an impressive pair of banks and ditches which cut off the end of the ridge. There is now little sign of occupation within the fort.

Return the same way to the road, go over the stile straight opposite, down through a former farmyard, and follow the farm track down to a railway bridge. Go under this, and immediately turn right along the path by the railway to reach the station.

Amenities

There are numerous pubs and cafes in Buxton and some in Chapel-en-le-Frith (a mile from the route). There is a licenced restaurant at Chapel-en-le-Frith station, and a pub (the Beehive) in Combs village.

The nearest public toilets are in Buxton, opposite the station; there are none at Chapel-en-le-Frith station.

Walk 6: Above Lamaload Reservoir

Start: at the car park at Lamaload reservoir (SJ975753). There is no other satisfactory parking place for the main route, but if you take the extension to Shining Tor and right along the ridge you will find a car park near to where you join the road at Pym Chair (SJ995768). All the lanes leading to Lamaload and Pym Chair are narrow and steep, so drive with care.

Distance: 3½ miles (alternatives 4½ to 5 miles).

Public transport: there are occasional buses, on Saturdays and summer Sundays only, between Macclesfield and Buxton (some of the Sunday buses continue to Bakewell and Chesterfield). These pass about a mile from the Lamaload car park, and also about a mile from Shining Tor (alight at the Shining Tor restaurant), making a one-way walk possible.

This walk explores the west side of the Shining Tor ridge, which separates the Goyt valley from the Cheshire plain. It runs through farmland and rough pasture, where many of the farmhouses have been abandoned. It can be extended to visit Shining Tor, the highest point in Cheshire. The walk is entirely in Cheshire (though the Shining Tor ridge forms the boundary with Derbyshire) and on the gritstone.

Most of the way is reasonably firm, but it is marshy near Thursbitch and after heavy rain it may not be possible to cross the stepping stones here.

The Walk

From the Lamaload car park turn right along the road for about 300 yards. Where the road turns sharply to the right, go through a stile by the gate on the left (footpath sign 'Burbage via Shining Tor') and follow the path up the narrow valley. The valley opens out at the site of Eaves Farm; its slight ruins can just be picked out near a large tree to the right of the path. Here turn left over a waymarked stile in a wall, aiming for a ruined barn, and cross a stile to the right of it. Continue in the same direction, aiming for a farm (Redmoor). The obvious grassy path to the top corner of the field is misleading, as the stile over the far wall is some way below it.

6. ABOVE LAMALOAD RESERVOIR

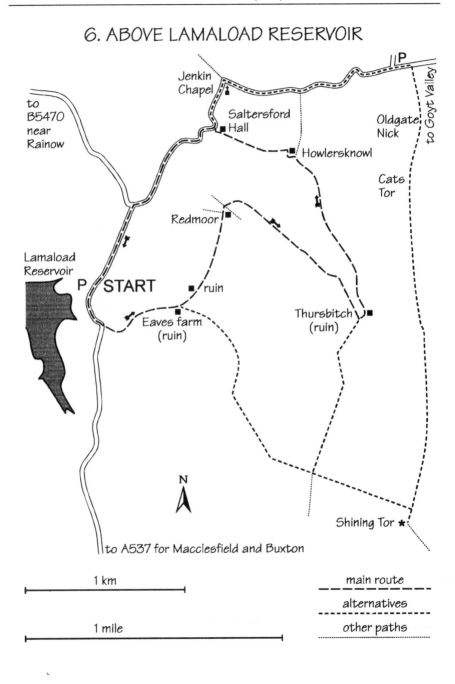

Pass (as waymarked) between the farm buildings and across the access road, through a nettle patch and over two stiles just to the left of a barn, and then bear right for a third stile. This takes you into a field which slopes down towards the brook. Go slightly left across this field, descending only slowly. The path is not clear, but the actual route is not critical because the next wall you have to cross is ruined. When the junction of two streams is visible, make for an inconspicuous stile in the fence rather to the right of the junction and cross the first stream directly below it. Go up the bank opposite and look for a path parallel to the second stream, but some way above it: do not take the faint path right up the ridge. Turn upstream along this path, with the stream on your left. At a reedy patch the obvious path is very muddy where it crosses a side stream, but there is a drier way a few yards uphill. At the next side stream, cross the wall by the stile.

The path now descends to the stream opposite the ruins of Thursbitch farm. Cross by the stepping stones and ascend to the ruins. Take the clear track which you will see running down the valley (to your left). This keeps well above the stream and climbs slightly, passing through two gates with stiles alongside. As the path levels out it becomes less clear, but beyond a single gatepost it runs along the right-hand side of a ruined wall. At the end of the wall the path becomes clear again, descending towards Howlersknowl farm.

As you approach the farm there is a well-marked stile to the right of a gate. Go through the gate, not over the stile. Just before a barn on the left, go through a gate on the left and follow the path which curves round the ridge and then descends it towards Saltersford Hall. Pass to the left of this building, noting the 1573 datestone, to reach the road. Turn left along the road, keeping left at the junction, to regain the car park in about three quarters of a mile.

Alternative routes

An alternative route to Thursbitch adds little to the distance, though it involves a stiff ascent and is likely to be wet in places after heavy rain. It gives the opportunity for a further extension to Shining Tor. To follow this route, do not go over the stile on the left at Eaves Farm (the ruined farm which is the first you come to) but carry on forwards to another waymarked stile, in a wire fence, and continue on the path which climbs steeply up the hillside. Beyond the next stile the path bears right; when it levels out it follows a fence on your right. The neat cone of Shutlingsloe is straight ahead at first, but the fence and path curve round to the left until you are facing Shining Tor. This is no more than the highest point on the long ridge, but can be distinguished by a small outcrop of rock just below the trig pillar.

The path undulates, passing over some wet ground, and crosses a stile in a wire fence. A cross path runs immediately beyond this fence, and you should turn left along it. If you wish, first visit Shining Tor by going straight ahead to the top of the ridge and then right along a path which used to be very wet, but is now being consolidated. You are now in Derbyshire, since the wall along the ridge forms the boundary (it used to run further east, along the Goyt Valley). Cross a stile to enjoy the view from the rocks just beyond the trig point which marks the top of Shining Tor, the highest point in Cheshire. Return the same way to the cross path by the wire fence. You will have added less than a mile to your route, but climbed an extra three hundred feet.

Follow the path parallel to the wire fence, but a few yards to its right (watch out for stones from an old wall). A stile takes you over one cross-fence; at the next cross wall, follow the path left past two large stone gateposts and then half-right, more or less along the contour. Beyond a ruined wall you can see the ruins of Thursbitch farm ahead; the path divides but either way will take you across the stream to the ruins, where you rejoin the main route.

If you do go to Shining Tor, you can walk nearly two miles along the

Shutlingsloe from Shining Tor

top of the ridge northwards to Pym Chair. This will give you a total of about 5 miles for the walk, with a stiff climb in the first mile and a half but mostly downhill or level after that. Just follow the ridge northwards from Shining Tor, with the wall on your left, until you meet the road. Turn left along it to Jenkin Chapel, a very simple building which could be mistaken for a farmhouse but for the low tower and the external staircase leading to the gallery. Turn left here and pass Saltersford Hall, and continue along the road to the car park as for the main route. This ridge walk gives you views into the Goyt Valley on your right as well as over the Cheshire plain to your left. The ridge forms the boundary between Derbyshire and Cheshire.

A further extension to this ridge walk, bringing it to 7 miles, is described in 'East Cheshire Walks' published by Sigma Leisure.

Amenities

The Cat and Fiddle on the A537 Macclesfield to Buxton Road is popular, possibly because it claims to be the second highest pub in England. There is a cafe on the same road half a mile nearer to Macclesfield than the Cat and Fiddle. The Setter Dog is three miles further down the main road to Macclesfield, marked 'Walker Barn' on the map. All these cater for the tourist trade. A quieter pub is the Stanley Arms in Wildboarclough. To reach it, turn right out of the Lamaload car park and cross the main road when you come to it; the pub is about half a mile further on, on your left. There are numerous pubs and cafes in Macclesfield and Buxton.

There are toilets and a picnic site at Lamaload reservoir, but no access to the water's edge.

Walk 7: The Upper Goyt Valley

Start: the car park near Derbyshire Bridge (SK019716). This is close to the A537 Macclesfield to Buxton road.

You can also park at the Goytsclough Quarry car park (SK011734) on the valley road: this will add about a mile to your walk. Or you can park at the kerbside near the end of the tarmac in Macclesfield Old Road in Burbage on the outskirts of Buxton (about a mile and a half from the centre), near Goslin Bar (SK036724). This is less than a quarter of a mile from the route of the walk.

Distance: $3\frac{1}{2}$ miles (alternatives $2\frac{3}{4}$ to $4\frac{1}{4}$ miles).

Public transport: From Buxton town centre there is a bus to Burbage (Level Lane) every two hours Monday to Saturday, but no Sunday service; this takes you within a quarter of a mile of the route of the walk at Goslin Bar.

There are occasional buses from Macclesfield to Buxton past the Cat and Fiddle, passing about half a mile from the Derbyshire Bridge car park, on Saturdays and summer Sundays only.

The walk starts in the narrow valley of the Goyt less than a mile from its source near the Cat and Fiddle inn. It follows the valley downstream; then climbs up a side valley and across the moor towards Buxton, with extensive views into the limestone country, before returning by the old course of the Macclesfield to Buxton turnpike. This is a rewarding walk for those interested in industrial history.

The walk is now entirely in Derbyshire, although the name 'Derbyshire Bridge' recalls the fact that the border with Cheshire used to follow the Goyt for much of its course. All the walk is in Gritstone country. About a mile is on a very quiet byroad. Most of the way is firm underfoot, but there will be a few muddy patches after wet weather.

You may find a free leaflet of Goyt Valley walks in the shelter by the Derbyshire Bridge toilet block; some of these walks are waymarked, and the route follows one of them for part of the way.

The Goyt Valley near Derbyshire Bridge

The Walk

Leave the car park by the narrow road which crosses the cattle grid and leads down the valley, with the infant Goyt on your left. You will notice shaly coal outcrops in the sides of the valley; at one time there were a number of small coal mines near here, though there is now little trace of them. You shortly cross Derbyshire Bridge, where you may notice a footpath on the right. This is not a right of way; it leads to grouse butts, and beyond this peters out in thick heather. A small footbridge a little further down the valley, without side rails, also gives access only to this path. Nearby you will see the mouth of a small tunnel close to river level; this was a drainage sough for coal mines up on the moor.

Follow the road for about a mile from the car park, then cross a substantial footbridge over the river. This is not marked on either the OS map or the walks leaflet, which is odd as it has been there for many years. (If you parked at Goytsclough Quarry, either walk up the road to this bridge or else cross the rebuilt packhorse bridge near the quarry and take the path up the other side of the river).

Now take the well-worn path which leads up the side valley, Berry Clough, with a small stream below on your right. In about half a mile this path crosses the stream by rough stepping stones; you are unlikely

7. THE UPPER GOYT VALLEY

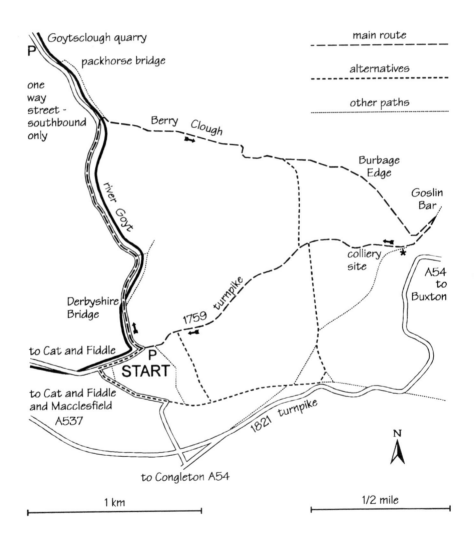

to have trouble here unless the weather has been very wet. In a few hundred yards the path forks at a small cairn and waymark post (the waymarked route goes right). Take the left fork and walk on to another waymark post and a stile in a wall, at the highest point of the walk where it crosses Burbage Edge.

Here the scenery changes dramatically. Behind you is the heather-covered moor; ahead the path crosses a reedy green field bordered by a belt of trees, and beyond the trees you are looking into the limestone country beyond Buxton. Buxton is hidden in the valley, but you can see Grinlow Tower ('Solomon's Temple') on a small hill ahead. Follow the clear path diagonally across the field, crossing a muddy patch half-way. The path turns left at the end of the tree belt, and joins an old road at a footpath sign and stile. Turn right up the road. (A short way down the old road from here is Goslin Bar, where there was once a toll gate, and beyond it is Burbage and the terminus of the local bus service from Buxton).

At this point you are surrounded by remains of the Peak District's industrial past. The old road itself was built as a turnpike in 1759 but superseded in 1821 by the present main road, which is less steeply graded although longer. You will find more details of these turnpikes in 'Peakland Roads and Trackways' by A.E. and E.M. Dodd (Moorland Publishing, 1980; unfortunately, now out of print).

Just below you is the route of the Cromford and High Peak railway, opened in 1831. The section from here to Whaley Bridge was closed in 1892, but the stump of the line near Buxton was retained to serve quarries until 1954 and the tracks ended just below you, where the bridge under the old turnpike has been partly filled in. On the other side of the little valley you can see where a short spur ran from this line to the Buxton Colliery, which closed about 1920, and if you walk a few yards towards it from the old road you will see that the ground has been much disturbed. You may be able to find the remains of the domed brick coke ovens. The site is described in detail in 'The Coal mines of Buxton' by Roberts and Leach (Scarthin books 1985).

Continue up the old turnpike road. It leads you back over the moor to the car park in just over a mile. As you climb the hill, much of the road surface has broken up; but there are a few stretches where it is still sound, made up of small broken stones, and this gives a good impression of what a main road was like at the beginning of the nineteenth century. The larger unbroken stones you see in places are the foundations which underlaid this smooth surface. A short way beyond the highest point of the road, on the right, is an illegible stone milepost.

Alternatives

You can shorten the walk by about three quarters of a mile if you fork right at the cairn and waymark post above Berry Clough, following the waymarked path (numbered 6). This will bring you to the old turnpike at its highest point; turn right for the car park.

For an extension which adds about three quarters of a mile, passing more traces of mining and another old turnpike road, go over a stile on the left just before the highest point of the turnpike, a few yards before the shorter route from Berry Clough joins it. A firm straight track, built to serve collieries, leads across the moor. (The OS map shows a right of way which cuts the corner, but it is difficult to follow on the ground).

The mine track passes many old run-in shafts associated with the Goyt colliery; in a couple of them you can see the top few courses of the shaft lining. Don't get too close, because the rubble which blocks the shaft may be held up only by rotting timber. As you approach the main road, the track forks. Take the right-hand branch (not shown on the OS map – the right fork shown further back is difficult to find), with a concrete grid base.

This track takes you almost to the main road, but after climbing the wooden fence beside the gate, turn right alongside the fence on a path which soon becomes a green track. This is evidently yet another former turnpike route, from its direct course and the stone-metalled surface which can be seen at the bottom of the ruts, though it is not mentioned in the Dodds' book. You can see behind you that it crossed the present main road (the 1821 turnpike) and ran to the right of the Terret plantation, on a spur of the hill, to join the Buxton to Leek road (another old turnpike). Ahead of you it drops to join the 1759 turnpike route a short way west of the Derbyshire Bridge car park, using the present byroad. As you reach the top of the hill you can just make out a very straight path forking left which lines up with the Congleton road; that is yet another old turnpike, which must have followed this line to join the road you are walking on before it was intersected by the 1821 road.

In wet weather it is best to follow this track till it reaches the byroad, and walk down it – turning right at the T junction – to return to the car park. Otherwise look out for a broken cross-wall on your right, and take the path which runs on the nearside of it; it will take you back to the 1759 turnpike and the car park. A parallel path beyond this, shown on the OS map, starts between a pair of blocked stone gateposts but is a little harder to follow.

Pastoral scene, Walk 7.

Amenities

The Cat and Fiddle inn is about a mile from the car park in the Macclesfield direction. It is popular with both motorists and walkers, and may be crowded at weekends. About half a mile beyond the Cat and Fiddle, on the right, is the Shining Tor restaurant, and if you fork left in front of it you will come in another mile to the Stanley Arms inn in Wildboarclough. In the other direction, there are many pubs and cafes in Buxton.

There are public toilets at the Derbyshire Bridge car park which are open all the year; in summer only there are also toilets at Goytsclough Quarry car park. There are also toilets just beyond the traffic lights by Burbage church on the road into Buxton.

Walk 8: Wilboarclough and the Cat and Fiddle

Start: Vicarage Quarry car park (SJ984706) in Wildboarclough, on a minor road which links the A54 with the A537.

If you prefer you can park at the Clough House car park (SJ987699), half a mile south down the valley in the fork of two roads, though this is more likely to be full on summer Sundays.

Distance: 5 miles (alternative 6 miles).

Public transport: there is a bus, morning and afternoon, from Macclesfield to Wildboarclough and back which passes both the suggested car parks, but it runs only on schooldays. On summer Sundays there is a morning bus from Macclesfield to Buxton via Wildboarclough, returning late afternoon.

From the attractive valley of Wildboarclough there is a stiff climb up Cumberland Clough onto the moors and along to the Cat and Fiddle, the second highest inn in England. From here your way follows a short length of an old coach road, and then a new concessionary path takes you back to Wildboarclough by way of Torgate.

This walk is entirely in Cheshire, on gritstone. One or two patches above Cumberland Clough and near Torgate will be wet after heavy rain, but not beyond what can be managed in boots.

About a mile of the walk is along the valley road in Wildboarclough; although this is a minor road it is quite busy at weekends. The suggested parking place splits the road section between the beginning and end of your walk.

The Walk

Turn right (downstream) along the road from the car park and follow it for half a mile to a road fork. Take the left fork and turn through a gate on the left, signposted to the Cat and Fiddle, opposite the top entrance of the Clough House car park. Another sign forbids motors; the track is legally a public road, which is why the OS map does not mark it as a footpath or bridleway.

8. WILDBOARCLOUGH AND THE CAT AND FIDDLE

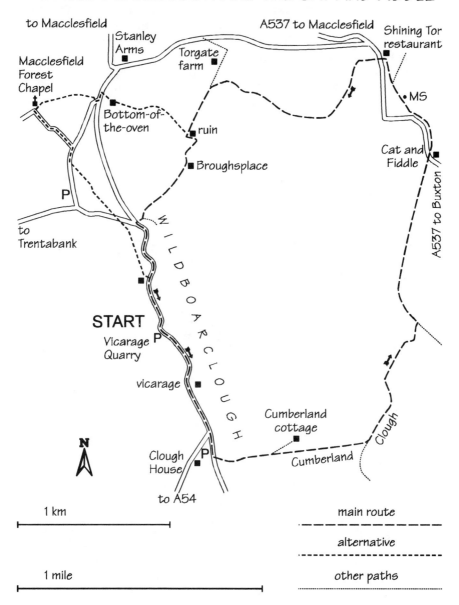

to Macclesfield

Stanley Arms

Torgate farm

A537 to Macclesfield

Shining Tor restaurant

Macclesfield Forest Chapel

Bottom-of-the-oven

• MS

ruin

■ Broughsplace

Cat and Fiddle

A537 to Buxton

P

to Trentabank

W I L D B O A R C L O U G H

START

Vicarage P Quarry

vicarage

Cumberland cottage

Clough House

P

Cumberland

Clough

to A54

1 km	main route
	alternative
1 mile	other paths

N

Shortly the track crosses a footbridge and continues upstream over a wooden stile beside a gate. The stream runs in a pretty wooded clough on your right. Notice a seam of poor quality coal in the other bank of the stream. Continue past the end of the wood and an iron gate; ahead of you on the skyline is the grass-covered spoil heap of an old coal mine.

Just beyond the gate is a junction of tracks, with a signpost; turn left on the track signed to the Cat and Fiddle. The stony track follows a stream, and shortly crosses it by a little bridge, wide enough for carts visiting another coal mine whose slight remains you pass shortly. Beyond this the path becomes rougher and steeper. The valley forks and the path follows the (usually) dry branch to the left, as the main valley is blocked by a small but attractive mossy waterfall. Shortly the path climbs up the right-hand side of its valley, goes through a gap in a ruined wall, and then on over grass with an old straight wall on the right. Behind this wall the stream, above the waterfall, runs in a steep clough. The view backwards opens out as you climb, but watch your step as there may be wet patches.

Beyond the end of the wall the path crosses the stream again. The stony path alongside the stream beyond the crossing leads to a very wet patch of peat; it is better to turn right on a green path which then curves round to the left. Both end up at another footpath notice, on a cross path with an old wire fence beyond it.

Turn left along this path. It rises slightly, and the radio mast by the Cat and Fiddle comes in sight. The rounded hill on the skyline to the left of the mast is Shining Tor, the highest point in Cheshire.

At the Cat and Fiddle, cross the busy main road. The inn is popular with both motorists and walkers and may be crowded at weekends. For a sheltered picnic spot, look out for a grassy depression – probably an old quarry – just to the left of the radio mast.

Inn sign at The Cat and Fiddle

Turn left in front of the inn, towards Macclesfield, and walk through the grass parallel with the road for 200 yards. Where the road bends left, go straight on along a firm path through a gate. On the right, just before the top of the slight rise, is a milestone telling you that it is 164 miles to London and 6 miles to Macclesfield. This track is in fact the original line of the turnpike road from Maccles-

Milestone on the old turnpike road near the Cat and Fiddle

field to Buxton, built in 1759 but superseded in 1823 by the present road which avoids steep gradients. The track you are on gives a good idea of what a main road was like in the days before tarmac. Incidentally, its route past the Cat and Fiddle made this the third highest turnpike road in England.

Ignore the path on the right and go on through a gate. Turn left beyond the next gate, just before the Shining Tor restaurant, and cross the main road and an inconspicuous stile directly opposite. A notice by the stile tells you that this is a concessionary path to Torgate. This path is fairly new, so in places it has not yet been trodden enough to be clear underfoot, but there are waymark posts at intervals.

Follow the wall, on your right, down to a dip (which may be wet). From here the path bears to the left across grass, more or less parallel to the electricity posts though you should keep above them to avoid a couple of wet patches. Where the little valley joins another, bear to the right. The path becomes clear, running halfway up the steep slope above the stream.

Beyond a stone step stile by a narrow gate the slope eases and the path is less clear again. You can see a wooden stile ahead in a wire fence just in front of a dip, left of Torgate farm on the hill beyond, but the path deviates to the right on its way there to avoid wet patches. Beyond the stile bear half-right, over a bridge and towards a wall. Follow the wall uphill, past the head of a wet depression. Then bear left away from it, up an obvious green track, to a waymark post on the skyline.

Beyond the post the path goes straight up the slope to join a right-of-way just in front of a wall, at a post which tells you that this is the other end of the concessionary footpath. Turn left along the track, and over a tall wooden ladder stile beside an iron gate. Continue along the track, which follows a wall on your right apart from cutting off a corner. There are signposts at intervals. Beyond a wall gap the track descends between walls, and turns left through the remains of farm buildings. This stretch of the path, passing an old stone trough, may be wet but you can bypass it on the right.

Beyond a wall gap the path runs alongside a stream as far as another ruined building, where it turns left over a footbridge and up to a narrow gate in front of a farm. Turn right along the farm track. Where it meets another in a quarter of a mile, turn right and then immediately left along the road. In half a mile you will find your starting point on the right.

Alternative routes

There is no opportunity to shorten this walk. You can add a visit to Macclesfield Forest chapel, a pleasant little church up on the hillside, at the cost of an extra mile. To do this, follow the main walk to the Cat and Fiddle and down the concessionary path to Torgate, and turn left as described for the main walk; but when you get to the farm ruins, turn right over a stile instead of left towards the stream. Turn right alongside the wall for 50 yards, then left along a grassy path in a slight depression. Cross the wall by a step stile on your left; then over a ladder stile on the left and across the field to a gate. Turn right alongside the wall, go through the farmyard of Bottom-of-the-Oven farm and down the track to the road.

Turn left along the road, fork right, and very shortly turn right up a rough walled track. This brings you, in a steep quarter of a mile, to the Forest Chapel. Turn left along the road just beyond it; turn right at a T junction, and about a hundred yards along beyond a bend cross a stile on your left. The path bears to the right down the hillside, crosses the road, and continues in the same direction to come out on the valley road just before a farm. Turn right along the road and you will be back at your starting point in a few hundred yards.

There are many pleasant walks in Macclesfield Forest; you can pick up a free map of them at the Trentabank car park.

Amenities

There is a riverside picnic field (though no seats) through the gate directly opposite the Vicarage Quarry car park.

The Crag Inn is a mile and a half down the valley. A short way beyond it is a cafe on the left. The Stanley Arms is a mile up the valley from the car park; if you turn right there you will find the Shining Tor restaurant a mile on.

The nearest public toilets are at the Trentabank car park (SJ962712) about two miles to the west.

Walk 9: Wildboarclough and Three Shires Head

Start: Clough House car park (Grid reference SJ987699), at the junction of the road running along Wildboarclough with a minor road which runs up to Crag Hall and the A54; entrances on both these roads.

If you prefer you can park in the layby on the A54 Congleton to Buxton road near Sparbent (SK001692), on the north side of the road (the left coming from Congleton). This is close to the route of the walk. If you intend to take the alternative route, use instead the layby on the other side of the A54 half a mile nearer to Buxton.

Distance: 4½ miles (alternative 5 miles).

Public transport: see walk 8.

The walk starts from Clough House in Wildboarclough, and climbs up Cumberland Clough for three quarters of a mile. It then follows a track to the A54 Congleton to Buxton road, crosses it and descends into the valley of the Dane to reach Three Shires Head. From here it climbs over the moor to re-cross the main road, and follows a quiet by-road back to the car park.

The walk is entirely in Cheshire and on the gritstone. Most of it is on a firm surface. A half-mile stretch across the moor may be wet after rain, but can be avoided at the cost of following the main road for half a mile. This is a fairly strenuous walk as it climbs twice from a valley over the moor.

The Walk

Go to the upper entrance of the Clough House car park, cross the lane and go through the gate opposite (signpost to Cat and Fiddle). The route is not shown as a public footpath on the OS map, since the track is legally a public road, but signs restrict the type of traffic that may use it.

After about 200 yards the track crosses the stream: continue up the wooded valley, which is Cumberland Clough. At the end of the wood

9. WILDBOARCLOUGH AND THREE SHIRES HEAD

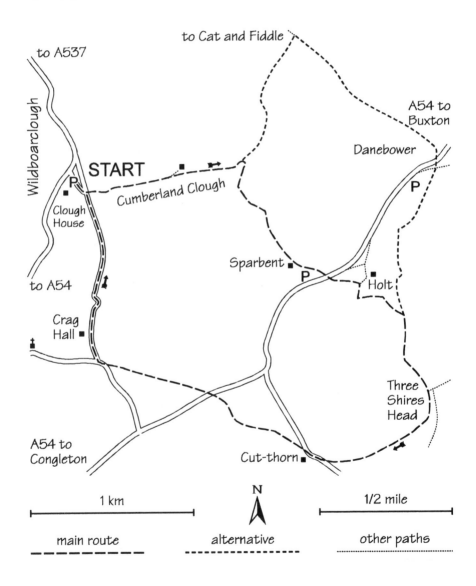

there is a gate and then a bridge – actually more of an embankment with a culvert through it. This is the site of one of several small coal mines which produced poor but usable fuel until cheaper transport from the richer coalfields made them uneconomic.

Ignore the track to the left signposted to the Cat and Fiddle; go over the bridge, and follow the track until it reaches the main road near a barn marked on the map as Sparbent. (The layby is a few yards down the road to your right).

Cross the road to a footpath sign opposite, and go down the steps. Cross a small field to a stile opposite, go over it, and turn left alongside the wall to a gate. Do not go through the gate, but turn right along a track. Beyond the next gate the track turns left alongside a small stream, then right again. At the next gate the track reaches the infant river Dane.

Follow the track down the valley for a quarter of a mile to the bridge at Three Shires Head. This is a picturesque spot, popular with photographers and picnickers. There is a waterfall below the bridge, and a side stream passes under a smaller bridge to join the Dane in Panniers Pool. Where the streams meet is the junction of three counties; Cheshire on your side of the Dane, Derbyshire opposite above the side stream and Staffordshire below it. This was an important meeting place of trackways before the main road was built higher up the valley side. If you look below the bridge you will see that it has been widened; it was built originally for pack-horse traffic.

Do not cross the bridge, but continue along the sandy track until it reaches a lane, with a cottage (Cut-thorn) opposite. Cross a stile just to the right of the cottage, and bear right up the middle of the field on a visible footpath, climbing gently. The path swings to the left and approaches a wall, forking twice. Take either the first or the second path to the right – they rejoin beyond the wall. Continue over the moor, passing a couple of wet patches, till you reach the main road again at a stile.

Cross the road and the stile opposite, and follow the clear path towards a small barn. There are several wet patches, the worst of which can be avoided. Pass to the right of the barn and down a field to a gate at the bottom. This gives onto a short track leading to a minor road. Turn right along this and turn right at the next junction, passing Crag Hall. This narrow lane brings you back to the car park in about three quarters of a mile.

Danebower

Alternative routes

After heavy rain the stretch of the route between Cut-thorn and Crag Hall may be wet, though not impassable if your boots are watertight. To avoid it, continue up the lane at Cut-thorn instead of going over the stile. At the main road turn left, and walk cautiously along it (there is a narrow grass verge) for about half a mile to a junction, where you take the minor road on the right to descend to the main route just before Crag Hall.

You can add about half a mile to the walk by going straight on up Cumberland Clough. Walk up to the gate at the end of the wood, as for the main route, but then turn left on the track signposted to the Cat and Fiddle. The stony track follows a stream, and shortly crosses it by a little bridge. The valley forks and the path follows the dry valley to the left. Shortly the path climbs up the right-hand side of its valley, goes through a gap in a ruined wall, and then on over grass with an old very straight wall on the right.

Beyond the end of the wall the path crosses the stream again. Turn right on a green path, which then curves left to another footpath notice, on a cross path with an old wire fence beyond it. Turn right along this path, which runs beside deep peat down the slight valley called Dane-bower Hollow.

At the main road go straight across, and descend steeply to a firm track. Here you can make a short detour left to look at the Danebower quarries, including a large water-filled pit with a waterfall where a stream enters it: return the same way. Otherwise turn right along the track, and then shortly leave it by a path which forks left (unless you parked in the layby on the A54, in which case continue along the track to the road and the layby is just ahead).

The chimney near this point is a relic of another coal mine. The engine-house was a short way down the hill, the flue sloping up the hillside to the base of the chimney. Across the valley you can see the old Reeve-Edge quarries. In dry weather you can scramble across the Dane to explore them, continuing to Three Shires Head by the quarry track towards Blackclough and then turning right down the side valley, without adding much to the distance; but after rain you will find it hard to cross the river.

The path slopes down to the Dane, here quite a small stream only a mile from its source, and runs alongside it past the remains of yet another coal mine. Watch out for a stile on the right, since the path which appears to continue alongside the river becomes impassable. There is no obvious path across the field; bear to the left across it, but keep well above the river to avoid the worst of the wet patches. Eventually a stile brings you onto a clear trackway. Turn left along it, and you are back on the main route; you will reach Three Shires Head in about a quarter of a mile.

Amenities

The Stanley Arms is a mile and a half up Wildboarclough from the car park; if you turn right there you will reach the main road opposite the Shining Tor Restaurant, and the Cat and Fiddle is half a mile to the right. The Crag Inn is about a mile down Wildboarclough; a short way beyond it, by a large layby on the left, is a cafe.

There are no public toilets close to this route; the nearest are at the Trentabank car park in Macclesfield Forest, about three miles off, and at Derbyshire Bridge in the Goyt Valley at a similar distance.

Walk 10: Wildboarclough and Quarnford

Start: the small layby opposite the bridge at Crag village in Wildboarclough (SJ983687). If this is full, there is a large layby a third of a mile down the valley at SJ980681 (this will add half a mile to your walk); or a few cars can park, carefully, at the roadside near the road junction at Crag Hall (SJ989688), which is on the route of your walk.

If you choose to take the extended walk you can use the Gradbach car park (SJ998662), which this extension passes; it is rarely full.

It is not possible to park on the A54 near either of the points where this walk crosses it, and it is difficult to park on the minor roads used in the walk.

Distance: 4 miles (alternative 4½ miles).

Public transport: there are no weekday buses other than the school bus, but on summer Sundays a bus leaves Macclesfield for Buxton via Wildboarclough in the morning and returns in late afternoon.

This walks starts in Wilboarclough, at the village which is properly called Crag although the name Wildboarclough is now used for the village as well as the valley. It follows an old packhorse track which linked textile mills at Crag and Gradbach, and then climbs back over the ridge to return by the minor road past Crag Hall.

Wildboarclough is an attractive valley, now entirely rural. Until quite recently there were substantial textile mills at Crag, but there is little sign of them now apart from a rather imposing house, once the mill offices, on the left of the road up to Crag Hall. Gradbach, in the parish of Quarnford, used to be a small industrial settlement round a textile mill. The mill is now a Youth Hostel; one cottage is a base for the Scouts, and the rest have vanished.

This walk is entirely in Cheshire (though the extension crosses into Staffordshire), on gritstone. Parts may be wet after heavy rain. About a mile and a half is on quiet minor roads.

Parking may be difficult on summer Sundays and Bank holidays, as Wilboarclough is a popular spot.

Barn at Higher Bongs

The Walk

From the bridge, walk downstream along the valley road towards the Crag Inn but go through a squeezer stile and over a footbridge on the left before reaching it. Follow any of the paths (the one alongside the wall on the right is easiest) to the top right-hand corner of the wood, and over a stile – the wet patch by the stile can be avoided. Go up the field, with the stream and wall on your right, and straight on through a wall gap by a waymark post; then bear half-right where the wall on your right ends to join a track at the bottom of the wood.

(If you start from the Crag Hall junction, walk down the hill past the church. Just before the telephone box, take a signposted lane on the left, which becomes a fenced footpath. At the end go straight on across the field. Then turn left at a waymark post through a wall gap, and bear half-right where the wall on your right ends to join a track at the bottom of the wood. There is a more direct way onto this track from the Crag Hall junction by Firs Farm, but it is very wet).

Turn right along the track. Follow it where it bears left round the end of the wood, pass left of the next wood and up the hill to a barn, and follow the track which bears right to reach the main road. Go straight across and up the hill for a short way to join a farm track; turn left along

10. WILDBOARCLOUGH AND QUARNFORD

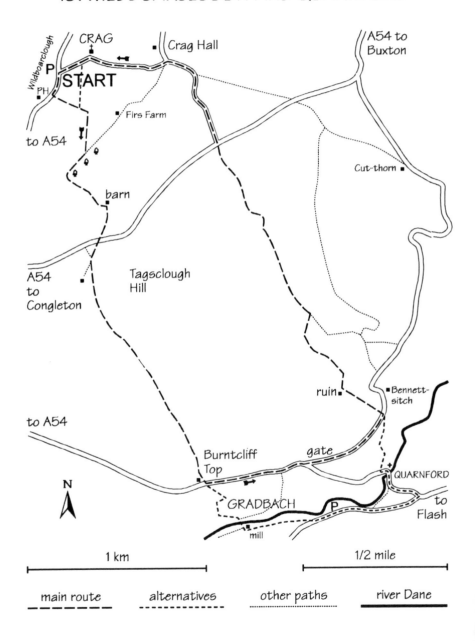

CRAG

Crag Hall

A54 to
Buxton

P

START

PH

Firs Farm

to A54

Cut-thorn

barn

A54
to
Congleton

Tagsclough
Hill

ruin

Bennett-
sitch

to A54

Burntcliff
Top

gate

QUARNFORD

N

GRADBACH

P

to
Flash

mill

| 1 km | 1/2 mile |

main route   alternatives   other paths   river Dane it, and keep left at the fork. Follow the track (an old packhorse route, and legally a public road – which is why it is not shown as a footpath or bridleway on the OS map) for a mile until it reaches a minor road at Burntcliff Top farmhouse – an old building which was once an inn. Notice the crest over the door.

Turn left along the road, and in a quarter mile fork left through a gate onto an unfenced minor road. Where it becomes walled there are footpath signs on both sides of the road. Follow the one on the left, up a walled track (the gate is marked 'Higher Bongs') past a ruined barn. Bear half-right to a waymarked stile, and follow the green path diagonally across the field, through a ruined wall and over a tiny stream. Turn left between the stream and a substantial wall, continuing over a step stile.

Where the wall on the right ends, cross a stile in the wire fence on the right and make for a ladder stile which is prominent on the skyline. Over this, follow a faint path along the top of a rock-strewn slope, parallel to the wall on your left, and cross another stile by a gate. Carry on along the green track, past a little quarry, towards Shutlingsloe whose top is now visible on the skyline. As the path starts to descend there is a good view across Wildboarclough towards Shutlingsloe, and a glimpse of the Jodrell Bank radio telescope over the ridge to the right of the concrete telecommunications tower on Croker Hill.

The path descends alongside a wall and comes out on the main road at a stile. Go down the minor road straight opposite. At the junction by Crag Hall, in a third of a mile, bear left and continue down the hill to your starting point.

Alternative route

You can add a pleasant half mile or so to this walk by continuing down the packhorse route from Burntcliff Top to Gradbach Mill and past the Gradbach car park and Quarnford chapel to regain the main route at the gate to Higher Bongs.

When you reach the minor road at Burntcliff Top, go straight ahead on an old track which zigzags down the steep hillside and crosses the Dane into Staffordshire by a footbridge close to Gradbach Mill. Walk past the front of the mill and turn left up the access road, past a ruined building which once provided lodgings for workers at the mill. Turn left along the road, past the car park. A short way beyond this there is a footbridge on your left. You can cross this, and walk along the river bank to join the road just short of the bridge by the chapel. However this path is usually very muddy, so you may prefer to continue along the lane to a junction, and then turn very sharp left along the road to the bridge.

Cross the bridge back into Cheshire and pass the chapel and a white house. Immediately beyond this, go up steps in the wall on your right and over a stile. Follow a clear path which climbs diagonally up the hillside and joins the road just before Bennettsitch. Go straight across, up a walled lane, and follow the directions for the main route.

Amenities

The Crag Inn, close to the start of the walk, supplies meals, although it may be a little up-market for some walkers. There is a cafe close to the large layby just down the valley from the Crag Inn.

Two and a half miles up Wildboarclough is the Stanley Arms. If you turn right here, there is a cafe where you join the main road and the Cat and Fiddle inn is a quarter mile further on. If you go down Wildboarclough from Crag, you reach a crossroads in just over a mile. Here you have three choices; left for the Rose and Crown (just beyond the hairpin bend), right for the Wild Boar and the Fourways Motel and restaurant, or straight on and then left at the church for the Ship inn at Wincle. My choice would be the Rose and Crown (except on Tuesdays) or the Ship.

The nearest public toilets are at the Trentabank car park in Macclesfield Forest (SJ962712).

Walk 11: Gradbach and Three Shires Head

Start: at the car park (SJ998662) at Gradbach, off minor roads which link the A54 Buxton to Congleton road with the A53 Buxton to Leek road. There are no other convenient car parking places; it is very difficult to park on the metalled road which forms part of the walk, and you should not park on grassland where the road is unfenced, though you may find room for a car or two at the end of the unfenced part at SK001667.

Distance: 4 miles (alternatives 3 to 4½ miles).

Public transport: none.

This walk takes you to Three Shires Head, a locally popular beauty spot where an old packhorse bridge crosses the Dane in a steep valley near its source. Derbyshire, Cheshire and Staffordshire meet at this point, and you will walk in all three. A waterfall below the bridge falls into Panniers Pool, where a side stream joins it below a smaller bridge. Photographers should note that in winter the bridges are in shadow except for an hour or two in the late morning.

The walk is manageable (in boots) after wet weather although there are some muddy patches. It is entirely in gritstone country, and you will notice that the rock is very red in this area.

The Walk

Leave the car park by the road you came along, or by a path which leads from the end of the car park to join this road near a footbridge. Do not go over the footbridge, but continue along the road to the junction and then turn sharp left. In about 100 yards go through a gate on the right which leads to a new house (footpath sign). Take the track which curves off to the right and go over a step stile (with FP sign) in the wall on your right.

Bear left and walk up the field, with the wall on your left. Carry on uphill through several gateways, keeping the wall close on your left. After a final steep rise the wall on your left ends; go straight ahead, and

11. GRADBACH AND THREE SHIRES HEAD

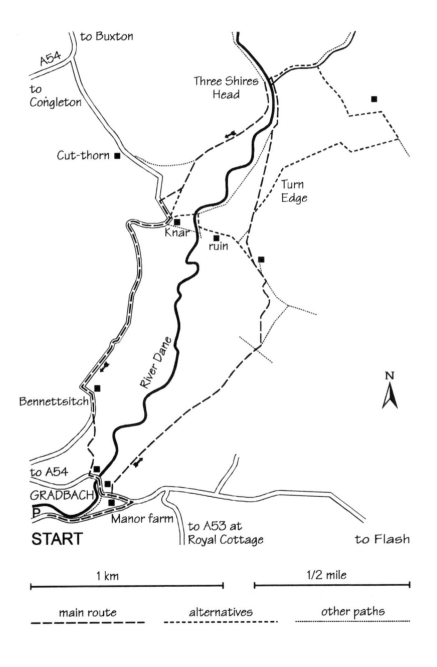

to Buxton

A54

to
Congleton

Three Shires
Head

Cut-thorn ■

Turn
Edge

Knar
ruin

River Dane

N

Bennettsitch

to A54

GRADBACH
P

Manor farm

START

to A53 at
Royal Cottage

to Flash

| 1 km | 1/2 mile |

main route   alternatives   other paths

you will come to a wall with a waymarked wooden stile, which you go over. Ahead of you, towards a cottage, is a ladder stile which you must also go over; but the direct path to it is often wet, and a deviation to the left may be drier. You will pass several round ponds or depressions surrounded by banks. These are probably the remains of bell-pits dug to extract poor quality coal from a shallow seam.

Beyond the ladder stile go diagonally left to the far corner of the field, aiming for a ruined barn by a prominent tree. At the corner, go through the gate on your right and bear left alongside the wall which curves towards the barn. Strictly speaking you should follow the wall to a squeezer stile on your left, go through it and turn right to a prominent squeezer stile by a gap in a wall; however, as all the walls are ruinous you can find a shorter route to this second stile.

Pass to the left of the barn and over a wooden stile in a wire fence, and you will shortly join a firm walled track. Turn left along it, and keep to the walled track – which becomes rough – where the wheel track forks right to an isolated house. Shortly beyond this you will see a ruined barn down the hill to your left, with a gateway above it; the shorter alternative walk goes that way, but for the main walk go straight on along the walled track.

As you come round a bend, a small wood comes in sight. The longer alternative walk forks right, at a footpath sign, into the wood; but for the main walk go straight on again. The path often has large puddles, but it is easy to bypass them to the right.

By an iron gate another path joins from the left, and you soon come to Three Shires Head. This was an important junction of packhorse routes before the turnpike road (now the A54) was built; if you look below the larger bridge you will see that it was originally too narrow for wheeled traffic. This is a lovely spot to be on a frosty winter morning, when the sun catches the bridge and the waterfall below it – after a cold spell the fall may be frozen solid.

Until now you have been in Staffordshire. Cross the first bridge which takes you briefly into Derbyshire, and then the second into Cheshire. Turn left along the stony track which climbs gently up the hillside. After rather less than half a mile, well after passing under electricity cables, fork left along a green path which leads to a way-marked wooden stile (adapted from an old gate). If the path is wet, it may be better to go a few yards further along the track and then scramble down to the stile.

There is an obvious green path from here, taking you through a waymarked gateway. At the gateway beyond this you have a choice of

Threee Shires Head

two rights of way. The slightly shorter, but wetter, one is through the waymarked squeezer stile on the left, then to a new wooden stile in front of Knar farmhouse. Alternatively you can follow the green path through the gateway and keep the wall on your left (with a slight detour round a wet patch) to a ladder stile.

Either stile brings you onto a very quiet tarmac road, and you turn left and follow the road for nearly a mile through a couple of gates and past several farms. The last of these (Bennettsitch) is at a sharp bend, and in a few yards the walls at each side of the road end. Immediately, at a footpath sign, take a green path forking left which slopes downhill among boulders. This leads gently down the hill, with the Dane in sight on the left. Pass to the right of a house, over a wooden stile and down a few steps to the road.

Turn left along the road, past the little chapel and over the bridge across the Dane which brings you back into Staffordshire. Just before the wall on your right ends, there is a gate and footpath sign. You can save a few hundred yards by taking this path, along the river bank to the footbridge over a side stream, where you turn right into the car park. However, the field is very muddy, especially at the far end where it is polluted by farmyard effluent; so you may prefer to continue along the road to the junction beyond the farm, and turn sharp right to return to the car park. If you do cross the field, you can avoid the wettest patch by going to the left of the wooden shed rather than straight towards the footbridge.

Alternative routes

If you don't want to visit Three Shires Head you can shorten the route by about a mile. After joining the walled track by the ruined barn and passing an isolated house, look out for a larger ruined barn down the hill and a gateway above it. Go down the field – there is a faint green path – and through the gateway. Go ahead down the track till you reach the river; turn right alongside it, over a bridge, and then up a very steep lane to Knar farm, where you turn left along the tarmac road which is the main route. (A short cut is shown on the OS map, but it may be very muddy).

You can lengthen the route by about half a mile by including Turn Edge. After passing the isolated house and going round a bend, take a signposted path which forks right at a footpath sign and climbs through a wood. At the top (which is Turn Edge) go over a stile on your right onto the heathery moor. Go straight ahead; the path is not very obvious, but when a slight valley appears the path follows the left edge of it.

Eventually a stile leads you into a field. Turn right for a few yards, then head left straight up the field to a barn; after a while you will have a wall on your right. There is a curious chamber built into the wall; if you can think of an explanation for it, let me know! At the barn you come onto a firm walled track; turn left along it.

Shortly the track comes to a gate leading to a house. Turn left just before the gate, down a stony walled track. This leads to a bridge over a little stream, beyond which you are in Derbyshire. Turn left alongside the stream and follow the track down to Three Shires Head. Go ahead over the larger bridge into Cheshire, and turn left; you are now back on the main route.

Amenities

If you turn left out of the car park and go straight ahead at the next three junctions, you will come in a couple of miles to the New Inn at Flash. Alternatively, if you turn sharp left at the first junction and go on for two miles you will reach the main road at the Rose and Crown inn at Allgreave (closed Tuesday lunchtime). There are of course many inns and cafes in Buxton.

There are no public toilets near the route. The nearest are at the Grin Low car park (SK047721), about six miles off near Buxton.

Walk 12: Wincle and Hammerton Knowl

Start: by the school next to Wincle church (SJ959661); there is a layby that will hold several cars.

It is not practicable to park on the A54 where you cross it at the Wild Boar inn, though if you propose to visit the pub you could probably use its car park. Likewise, if you intend to take the longer 'alternative route' you could park at the Ship Inn if you will be visiting it – go straight down the hill from the church instead of turning past the school, and the inn is about half a mile down on the left. There is a little roadside parking here, and more where the road widens about 200 yards further down the hill, at Danebridge.

Distance: 4 Miles (alternatives 3, 4½ miles).

Public transport: none.

This walk climbs from the Dane valley to pass behind the rounded hill of Hammerton Knowl, returning past the Wild Boar inn. Only a few hundred yards are along roads (mostly quiet), the rest on footpaths or farm tracks. There are good views across to Shutlingsloe and the Roaches. The walk is entirely in Cheshire, and on gritstone. It is passable after rain, although there are some muddy stretches.

The Walk

From the layby near Wincle Church, turn eastwards (away from the road junction) and walk along the road for 200 yards, past Hammerton Farm on your left. Turn right along a tarmac farm road. This is level at first, then drops. Where the tarmac track turns right to Bartomley Farm, the way ahead, though a right of way, is a dead end which leads only down to the river Dane. So turn left, along a path which climbs gently along a slight terrace which is in fact the remains of an old wall.

Where the path forks, take the left fork and continue just above a steep bank with, later, a wood and a wire fence on your right. Cross a wooden stile and go straight on, through a gap in the wall just right of a holly tree, and another wooden stile between two hollies. Beyond this

12. WINCLE AND HAMMERTON KNOWL

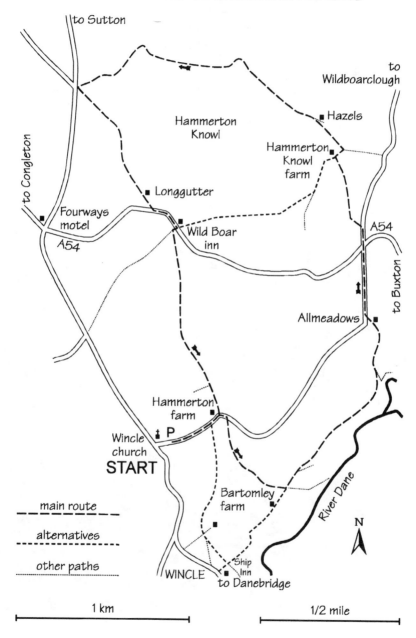

to Sutton

to Wildboarclough

to Congleton

Hammerton Knowl

■ Hazels

Hammerton Knowl farm

■ Longgutter

Fourways motel

A54

■ Wild Boar inn

A54

to Buxton

Allmeadows ■

Hammerton farm ■

Wincle church

P

START

Bartomley farm

River Dane

N

Ship Inn

WINCLE

to Danebridge

main route

alternatives

other paths

1 km

1/2 mile

your way continues as an obvious green track above a retaining wall, curving left. From here you get a good view of the junction of the Dane and the Wildboarclough Brook below you, and the conical peak of Shutlingsloe ahead. A track which zigzags up the hill to join you comes from Folly Mill, whose ruins (on private ground, and unsafe) are hidden in the wood on the right.

Cross a wooden stile and approach Allmeadows farm, where there are two gates. Take the left-hand one, as waymarked, and go straight ahead along the short drive to the road. Turn right along it and go straight on at the crossroads.

In a hundred yards there is a gate on the left, with a footpath sign. Go through it and follow the track up the hill. You will come shortly to three gates; take the middle one, on your right, and walk almost level along the field with the wall on your right. The next stile is in a wire fence a few yards up from the wall. Now aim slightly uphill towards a gate by the lowest building of Hammerton Knowl farm.

At the gate you have the option of shortening the walk by a mile, by going straight to the Wild Boar Inn (see 'Alternative routes'). Otherwise, ignore the waymark directing you through the gate; the right of way is shown on the map as going through the farm buildings, but that way is blocked by a barbed wire fence. So follow the fence to the right of the

Shutlingsloe from Hammerton Knowl

gate, past the bottom of the farm premises, and then aim slightly uphill to a gateway by two poles (one with a transformer half way up it). Beyond this, go more or less level and through an iron gate, which takes you behind Hazels farmhouse. The next gate brings you out on a concrete farm road; turn left along it.

Follow this road for nearly a mile as it winds round the back of Hammerton Knowl, passes through a shallow valley and climbs again to a byroad. Here you turn sharply left along a signposted track instead of joining the road, and descend slightly to a stile and gate. Go over the stile and follow the obvious track, which rises slightly beyond the next stile and gate to go round the end of a small hill, and then reaches a wooden stile just beyond a rushy patch. Beyond the stile, the sunken lane on the left has become a stream so continue across a rather wet field alongside it. Go through an iron gate and down the lane between farm buildings to the main road. Walk carefully left along it for a hundred yards to the Wild Boar inn.

Cross the road to a pair of gateways opposite the inn. Do not go over the stile but go through the gate on your left. There is no obvious path, although there may be wheelmarks, but aim more or less along the ridge, keeping to the right of it, until you see a derelict wall pointing straight

Ladder stile near the Wild Boar Inn

towards you. Go left of this and follow it down to join a farm track, which is concrete from this point.

Where the concrete track turns sharp right, go straight ahead over a wooden stile and down a hollowed track. This can be very muddy; there is a drier route above the bank on the left. Join the road at an iron gate, and turn right along it for 200 yards to your car (for the Ship inn, take the path on the left just past the bungalow).

Alternative routes

You can shorten the walk by nearly a mile if you go straight to the Wild Boar inn from Hammerton Knowl farm, instead of going round the back of Hammerton Knowl. To do this, go through the gate with the waymark and turn left, through another gate, along the farm drive. In 200 yards, when you are nearly opposite a wall corner on your right, leave the drive and fork slightly right, with the wall on your right. Where there is a kink in the wall, go through a facing stile and continue with the wall on your left. At the next gateway, ignore the obvious track and continue, climbing slightly, alongside slight remains of an old wall. This is joined by a fence; continue to a step stile in the field corner and on with the fence on your left. This leads to a waymarked ladder stile a few yards above the next field corner. From here you can see the Wild Boar inn across the next field; make for it, and cross a stile on its left to reach the main road and the route of the main walk.

You can join the main route from the Ship Inn (or from Danebridge, a further two hundred yards down the hill); this will add about half a mile to the walk. Walk a few yards uphill from the inn and go up the signposted steps on your right, across a drive, and through a kissing gate, then on up the field to a footpath signpost. Go straight on, past a waymark post, to a stile under a tall larch tree. An obvious path leads down into the wooded Hog Clough, across a stone slab bridge, and up to a stile on the other side. Continue up the field, keeping near the wall on your left, past the front of Bartomley farmhouse; then cross a stile (signposted) on the left just before the barn. Go right, round the corner of the barn, and along the farm track. Where this turns left, go straight ahead; you are now on the main route.

When you reach the road after walking down the track from the Wild Boar inn, turn right; but instead of going on towards the church look for a step stile and footpath sign on your left, immediately past the entrance to a bungalow. (After heavy rain it would be wiser to continue along the road to the church and turn left at the road junction). Follow the valley down, going through a stile just to the left of the stream, and then cross the stream to another stile. There is no bridge, but the stream is easy to cross unless it is running high.

Beyond the stile, bear left alongside the fence, turning left with it where it passes a stone trough. Eventually it bears right, away from the valley, and you come to a wooden stile. Cross this and go just right of the barn to cross another stile and a drive. Opposite, at the end of a very short track, are two gates. Go over the stile beside the left-hand gate, and straight down the field to a stile just right of a row of tall trees. Just beyond this is the footpath signpost you passed on the outward journey; turn right to reach the road, and the Ship Inn is just to your left.

Amenities

You can eat at the Ship Inn (leave your boots outside!), which is about half a mile down the road from Wincle church, or at the Fourways Diner which is about a mile up the steep hill from the church, just left at the crossroads. Or go straight on at this crossroads to reach the Hanging Gate in another two miles, or right at the crossroads for the Wild Boar (a Real Ale pub, though the food is a bit pricey) in half a mile. Or you can continue along the road past the school, turn right on the A54 at the crossroads, and the Rose and Crown is a quarter mile on just past a hairpin bend.

The nearest public toilets are about four miles north, at the Trentabank picnic area (SJ962712). There are also toilets at the Timbersbrook picnic site towards Congleton (SJ895628) and Derbyshire Bridge towards Buxton (SK009716).

Walk 13: Danebridge and Lud's Church

Start: the walk starts just west of the bridge over the river Dane at Danebridge (SJ965652). There is no car park, but the road near the bridge is wide and a number of cars can be safely parked at one side. Danebridge is a popular spot, so parking places may be short on a summer Sunday.

There is no other convenient parking near to the main route. If you take the longer extension to Roach End there is a little room to park on the verge there (SJ996645), but this becomes full at weekends and is reached only by narrow lanes.

Distance: 4 miles (alternatives 4¾ to 5¾ miles).

Public transport: there is no convenient bus service.

This walk takes you up the Dane Valley, passing the confluence of the Wildboarclough brook. Above this point the valley narrows and in places the river runs in a rocky gorge, though trees make this difficult to see in summer. Climbing out of the valley, the route passes Castle Rock, with an optional visit to the remarkable ravine called Lud's Church. It then climbs over the ridge of Back Forest to descend by Hanging Stone and through the woods back to Danebridge.

The walk is in Staffordshire, apart from the first and last few yards; the river Dane marks the boundary. It is on gritstone. Parts of it can be muddy in wet weather, so it is best after a dry or frosty spell, but the views are best when the leaves are off the trees. The only road walking is a few yards on a quiet byroad from your parking place.

The Walk

Note that the sketch map is drawn with East at the top.

Walk across the bridge over the Dane and turn left (upstream) on a well-worn path. Ignore a stile on the right and continue along a muddy riverside meadow, shortly bearing slightly uphill to a stile on your right. Cross the stile and turn left. There is a clear path through rocky woodland for about half a mile. At the end of the woodland go straight

13. DANEBRIDGE AND LUD'S CHURCH

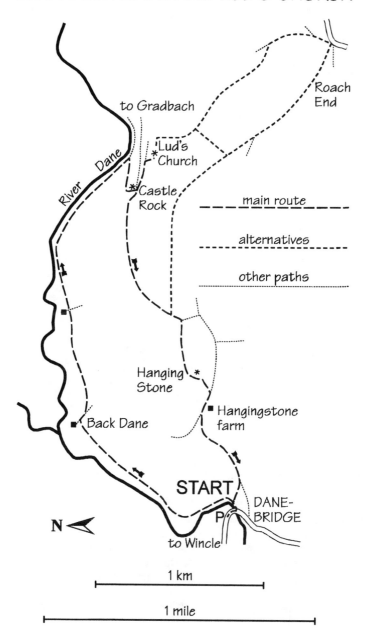

ahead, aiming just to the right of Back Dane cottage. From this point there is a good view across the valley to the lower end of Wildboar-clough, whose brook joins the Dane here, with the conical top of Shutlingsloe beyond.

Go a few yards right up the track from the cottage and then take a faint path left, more or less following the contours; it does not matter if you follow a different route across this field, so long as you end up at a gate and stile through a wire fence alongside an old wall. Beyond the stile the path is clear as it contours round the heads of two little side valleys and then goes just to the right of a renovated farm house. Its route here is clearly marked by fence posts. Beyond the farm it rises slightly and then falls left to a stile with a sign that tells you that you are entering the Roaches Estate nature reserve; this is owned by the Peak Park authorities.

After descending steeply to river level the path climbs again into scrubby woodland, and is very clear. The river Dane is close on your left. Its valley narrows into a rocky gorge in places, although this is difficult to see if there are leaves on the trees. After nearly a mile of woodland the path comes out on a more substantial made-up pathway sloping down the hillside, with a footpath sign pointing back the way you have come. (If you turn left here you come in half a mile to the Gradbach Youth Hostel, and in another half mile to the Gradbach car park).

Turn sharp right up this path, which is clear and well-used although, curiously, not shown on the OS map. The path climbs steadily for a quarter mile and then bears left under Castle Rock, a large outcrop which is a popular scrambling ground for small children. Behind the rock is a small clearing, and at the back of it a footpath signpost. From here your eventual route is to the right, but first visit Lud's Church if you have not been there before.

There are two paths left from the signpost. Take the narrower right-hand one, which slopes gently uphill. In about 200 yards take an inconspicuous path on the right which leads you straight into Lud's Church. This is a deep narrow cleft in the rock, its sides dripping with moss and ferns. Tradition says that the Lollards, a dissident religious group, held services here at the beginning of the 15th century. Eventually they were surprised by soldiers and the preacher's granddaughter was shot in the confusion. For those with literary interests, it has been suggested that this was the 'green chapel' in the medieval poem 'Sir Gawain and the Green Knight'. The cleft (and others nearby) started as vertical fault lines in the rock, which widened as the rock on one side slipped slowly downhill towards the river.

Retrace your steps to the clearing behind Castle Rock and go straight on, on a well-worn path with the valley on your right. The path climbs and curves left to reach the ridge of Back Forest at an iron gate and footpath signpost. Go through this gate and look out for a stone stile in the wall above you on the right, a few yards beyond the gate. Cross this and follow a faint path along the ridge to a stile in the wall opposite. A short way beyond this the path bends left onto the crest of the ridge and you will find yourself above Hanging Stone, a large projecting mass of rock.

Take the steps down beside the rock, to its right. There are two memorial tablets on the rock, put there by the Brocklehurst family who lived at Swythamley Hall nearby. Now bear right and descend to the farm road. Pass Hangingstone farm on your left. Just beyond the farm, a signposted path forks left and leads to a stile in the wall. Cross this and go straight across the field, aiming first for an isolated lump of rock and then for a post. Beyond this, look for a stile in the wall below on your right and cross it into woodland. A clear and well maintained path, with steps in places, leads through the wood and eventually down beside a stream to a stile. (The last part of this path is not shown on the OS map, but the older route is less easily found and brings you out a hundred yards further up the road). Turn left along the path and right over the bridge to your starting point.

Alternative routes

You can add three-quarters of a mile to your walk by continuing right through the cleft of Lud's Church (it may be muddy at the bottom), climbing up the rough steps at the other end and continuing along the path. Be careful if you stray from the path, because there are other clefts and some are hidden by the undergrowth. After about a quarter of a mile you will find a post indicating a concessionary footpath to your right. Follow this up the hill to the ridge, and turn right. Wallabies, escaped long ago from Swythamley Park, are occasionally seen in this area. After a very pleasant half mile you will descend to a track at a gate and footpath sign. Turn left through the gate, and then through a stile in the wall up on your right, and you are back on the main route.

To add yet another mile, do not take this concessionary path but continue through the wood for another half mile till you meet a cross path and footpath sign. Turn right and climb through heather and bilberries, on a clear path, to a track – where you turn right – and up to the road at Roach End (at summer weekends you may find an ice cream van here). Turn right, but don't take either the road through the gate or a farm track to the right. Instead go through a stile on your right to the top of the ridge and walk along it. Continue (on another concessionary path not shown on the OS map) along the ridge, ignoring a path that slopes down on the left with a wall, and you will pass the top of the concessionary path used in the shorter extension. Carry on to the gate and signpost as before.

Amenities

The Ship inn at Wincle is about a quarter of a mile up the road, on the Cheshire (west) side, from your starting point. If you go past it and turn right at the church, then right at the main road, you will come to the Rose and Crown (closed Tuesday lunchtime) just beyond a hairpin bend. Or go straight on at the church, and the Fourways Diner is close to the next crossroads; if you go straight on at this crossroads you will come to the Hanging Gate in a mile and a half.

The nearest public toilets are four miles south at the Tittesworth Reservoir car park (SJ994603), where there is also a cafe in the summer, or at the Trentabank car park (SJ962712) in Macclesfield Forest a similar distance north.

Castle Rock

Walk 14: Tittesworth and Upper Hulme

Start: the public car park at the north end of Tittesworth reservoir (SJ994604), a quarter mile east of Meerbrook village. There is a charge for parking.

There is limited free parking at the roadside half a mile further west, by Meerbrook village hall (SJ987608); this is about half a mile from the main route of the walk, or a hundred yards from the alternative route. You can park at the roadside near Upper Hulme, on a short loop of road which is now bypassed by the A53 main road. Or you can use a layby on the minor road below the Roaches, near where the route crosses it, but you will not find space there at weekends.

Distance: 3½ miles (alternative 4 miles).

Public transport: there are three or four buses a day (weekdays and Sundays) from Leek to Buxton via Upper Hulme, passing close to the route of this walk (take the lane down to Upper Hulme and turn right up a concrete track just before the bridge), and there are additional Monday to Friday buses from Leek to Upper Hulme. On Sundays (and bank holiday Mondays) there are buses from Hanley and Leek to the Tittesworth car park; few in winter, more in summer.

A free minibus service runs on summer weekends between the Tittesworth Reservoir car park and the layby just below the Roaches and Hen Cloud.

To the west of the Leek to Buxton road is the long ridge of the Roaches, with the rocky outcrops of Hen Cloud and Ramshaw Rocks closer to the road. Below the Roaches lies the Tittesworth reservoir. This walk starts from the large car park at the reservoir and follows a quiet route to the tiny industrial hamlet of Upper Hulme, then passes behind Hen Cloud to return by another route. Hen Cloud and the Roaches can easily be climbed from the low saddle between them – they make excellent scrambling grounds for children. A few parts of the route may be wet after heavy rain.

This walk is entirely in Staffordshire, on gritstone. There is about half a mile of road walking, along a minor but fast road which forms the boundary of the Peak District National Park; the car park is just outside the Park but the rest of the walk is within it.

Barn between Tittesworth reservoir and the Roaches

The Walk

Note that the sketch map is drawn with East at the top.

Leave the Tittesworth reservoir car park by the main entrance and turn right along the road for a quarter of a mile. Turn left along a gravel lane just before a house on the left of the road. In a quarter of a mile the lane turns left; your way is straight ahead over a stile. After a hundred yards or so you will see a handrail in the hedge on the left. Follow it down to a stream and up the other side (the stream seems to have taken over a sunken lane). Continue with the stream on your right until you approach a farm. Just beyond the stile is a signpost which sends you left up the field, then another which directs you right along a lane. Continue past the farm to the road, and turn right along it, down a hill and between industrial buildings into the hamlet of Upper Hulme.

At the bottom of the hill, cross the bridge and then turn left off the road to go straight up a concrete track. (A footpath shown on the OS map to the left of the stream appears now to be lost). The concrete ends but the track continues to the ruins of Dain's mill. Keep out – the building is dangerous – but pass between the mill and a small building on its left which was a drying kiln for the grain. Continue up the valley with the stream on your right, past a large crop of manholes. When you

14. TITTESWORTH AND UPPER HULME

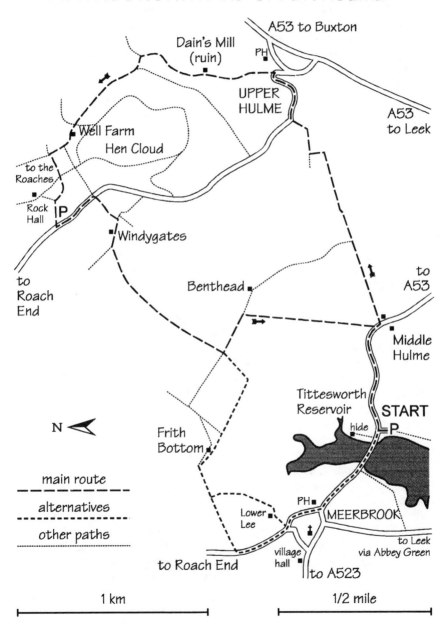

A53 to Buxton

Dain's Mill (ruin)

PH

UPPER HULME

A53 to Leek

Well Farm
Hen Cloud

to the Roaches

Rock Hall

P

Windygates

to Roach End

Benthead

to A53

Middle Hulme

Tittesworth Reservoir

START
P

N

Frith Bottom

hide

Lower Lee

PH

MEERBROOK

to Leek via Abbey Green

to Roach End

village hall

to A523

--- main route

······ alternatives

········· other paths

1 km

1/2 mile

reach a marshy section of the path with a small barn ahead, bear left just before the marsh to a gateway and cross the stile on its right.

Go up the field to a farm road, and turn right along this to Well Farm. Follow a rather tortuous, but signed, route to the right of the farmhouse, then left between it and the farm buildings, right past the lower end of these, and across a field to a stile by a wooden shed. Go on over more stiles till you reach open ground at the end of the Roaches, and turn left along a grassy lane. From here you can make an excursion either left to Hen Cloud or right to the Roaches (it is a mile along the ridge to the summit), returning the same way. Follow the track to the road, by a large and popular layby (at summer weekends you may find an ice cream van). This is the destination of the minibus service from the reservoir car park.

Turn left along the road for about 300 yards, then right over a stile. The OS map shows alternative paths to this point from Well Farm, but they are less easy to follow than the one I have described. Go down the field to join a farm road just to the left of some trees. Turn right and pass through Windygates farmyard, with a fine 17th century farmhouse on your right. Go straight on beyond the buildings for a few yards, to avoid a muddy patch, then take a track which leads off to the left. Near the bottom of the field branch to the right of this track to go through a gate just to the right of an iron Dutch barn. Keep the hedge on your left to the next gate, and continue in the same direction with the hedge now on your right to a stile.

Turn left after crossing the stile (the alternative route described later goes straight ahead), and follow the fence; there are waymarks most of the way from here. At the end of the field, go through a stile just to the left of a large holly bush. This stile has two waymark arrows; your way is half-right to a stile in the hedge (unless you parked at Upper Hulme or near the Roaches, in which case you can save a quarter of a mile by taking the path straight ahead, past Benthead farm, and following the farm road for a quarter mile until it turns sharp right. Here turn left over a stile, and you are back on the main route). From here you bear rather to the right across the field to another stile, and continue in the same direction – almost due south – across a number of fields until you reach the road. Some of the stiles are hard to see from a distance, but all are near the electricity lines. (The OS map shows several bends in the right of way, but since there are good stiles on the direct line I assume that the farmer prefers you to use it). Turn right along the road for a quarter mile to the car park.

Alternative route

This is slightly longer than the main route, but takes in Meerbrook village and the Lazy Trout inn and passes near the parking space at the village hall.

About half a mile beyond Windygates, go straight ahead instead of turning left after crossing the stile. From here the route follows one of the 'Staffordshire Moorland Walks' and there are some waymarks. The path crosses a stile just right of a barn and continues ahead to another stile a few yards to the right of an iron gate.

Just beyond this stile the route crosses a little stream (muddy patch, but there is a stepping stone) and turns right, in the direction shown by the footpath sign, diverging from the hedge on the right to reach a waymarked stile. It continues across the next field, aiming left of the farm and keeping just right of a dry ditch, to another stile which leads into a fenced path with boardwalk over the wettest patches. When this path reaches a farm road, turn left along it.

From here the easiest way is along the track to the road, then left along it to the Lazy Trout inn (a narrow turning on the right leads straight to the village hall) and left again for the reservoir car park. You can cut off a corner, at the expense of crossing some very wet patches, by turning left over a stile immediately past the cattle grid, going shortly over a stile in the fence on the left, and then following this curving fence towards a farmhouse. Pass in front of the house (derelict when last seen) to reach the road. Turn left for the Lazy Trout and left again for the car park.

Amenities

There are toilets, a cafe, covered picnic space, a children's play area and a small visitor centre at the far end of the reservoir car park. Boats on the reservoir are for anglers only.

The Lazy Trout inn is a quarter mile to the left as you leave the car park, and the Three Horseshoes a mile to the right at the main road junction at Blackshaw Moor. The Rock Inn at Upper Hulme (on the loop cut off by the main road, above the turning to the village) offers lunchtime food at weekends only. If you take the minor road which runs west of the reservoir towards Leek, you will come to the Abbey Inn at Abbey Green. This is one of my favourites though often busy. There are several inns and cafes in Leek.

Bird watchers may be interested in a hide, open to the public, which is reached by a path beside the upper part of the reservoir almost opposite the car park entrance.

Walk 15: Upper Hulme and The Morridge

Start: park at the roadside (SK013610) near the Rock Inn on a short loop of road, formerly part of the A53 Buxton to Leek road but now bypassed, just above the little village of Upper Hulme. There is little traffic, though you should leave room for the occasional bus and farm wagon.

You can if you prefer park near the Mermaid inn (SK037604) up on the Morridge; if you do this the last part of your walk will be uphill – something I try to avoid! There are several safe parking points on the verge. You will find your path just to the left of the inn car park.

Distance: 3½ miles (alternative 4½ miles).

Public transport: there are several buses a day along the Leek to Buxton road, stopping at Upper Hulme, and a single bus on Wednesdays only from Hartington and Longnor via the Mermaid inn to Leek and back.

This walk takes you from the Buxton-Leek road up to the Mermaid inn, near the highest point of the long ridge called the Morridge. It returns by another route which passes an attractive little ravine and crosses the infant river Churnet. This is almost unknown country, and you are unlikely to see another walker.

The walk is entirely in Staffordshire, on gritstone. About 400 yards of it are along a main road, but there is an adequate grass verge.

It would be wise to avoid this walk after heavy rain; it should not be particularly muddy, but it may be difficult to cross the stream between the Mermaid and Little Swainsmoor.

The Walk

Note that the sketch map is drawn with East at the top.

Walk downhill along the loop road, back to the A53 main road, and turn right along it. After 200 yards, just beyond the bridge, turn left along a farm track, and keep bearing left to reach the track to Hurdlow farm. (There is a short cut which avoids the main road, but it is likely to be muddy and is more difficult to follow. It starts from the loop road

15. UPPER HULME AND THE MORRIDGE

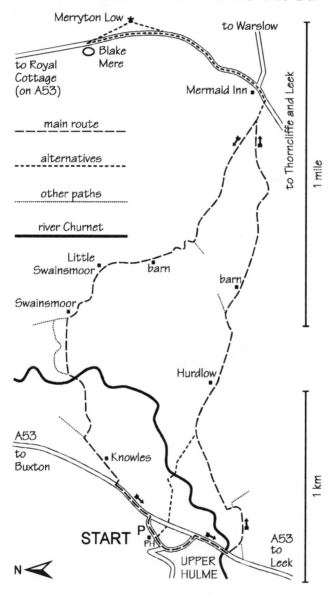

Merryton Low

to Warslow

Blake Mere

to Royal
Cottage
(on A53)

Mermaid Inn

to Thorncliffe and Leek

——— main route

········· alternatives

.... other paths

river Churnet

1 mile

Little
Swainsmoor
barn

barn

Swainsmoor

Hurdlow

A53
to
Buxton

Knowles

1 km

START
P
PH

A53
to
Leek

UPPER
HULME

N

and passes through a farmyard just below the inn, on the other side of the road. Go under the main road, then slightly left towards the far corner of the field. Just right of this is a rickety stile. Over this, turn left through a muddy patch and then bear down the steep slope. At the nearest point of the stream you will see a footbridge. The area in front of it is very wet, even in summer; the best route is by a large log. Once over the bridge, head up the field to pick up the Hurdlow Farm track, and turn left along it).

Pass straight through Hurdlow farmyard and follow the track up the next field, with the wall on your left. You can see the Mermaid inn on the skyline straight ahead. After a slight kink where the track crosses a little valley, continue up the track until the top of the field comes in sight with a barn beyond it. Leave the track and head for a stile in the top corner of the field, to the right of the barn. Cross it and head diagonally left across the field; aim not for the gateway you can see on the skyline, but below it towards a stile in the corner of a field beyond a little valley. You will find a track leading across the valley and up to the stile.

Beyond the stile, the OS map indicates that the right of way makes a beeline for the Mermaid inn (you can see only the chimneys by now). In fact you should bear rather more uphill, aiming for the right-hand end of a small ridge, to find an easy crossing of a deep gully. Continue in the same direction, over grass with a faint path at times. When the inn comes in sight again, make straight for it.

As you approach the Mermaid inn, you join a clear track coming from your left. This is your way back, so turn left down it (after visiting the inn if you choose). The track becomes indistinct in places, but your way leads down the crest of the ridge with the fence a short way to your right. Later the track becomes clear again. Ignore a stile on your right and continue along the track as it turns left to cross a side stream. (The continuation of the track beyond the stream is not a right of way, and is not shown on the OS map). Just before the crossing, go through a gate on the right, waymarked with blue bridleway arrows, and turn left downhill. The path is not clear, but the gully on your left is very attractive and you will see it best if you keep near the brink of the steep slope. Eventually you join a track which winds down to the junction of two streams. Pick your way across the one on your right, which is not difficult unless the level is high, and go through the gate opposite.

An old track, recognisable by its stone banking, winds up the slope to the left. When you can see a barn, aim for the gate just to the right of it, by an electricity pole, and cross the stile beside it. From here there is an obvious track across the field to the nearest farm (Little Swainsmoor). Pass to the right of the nearest building to reach the farm road, and follow this past Swainsmoor farm. Just beyond this the right of way cuts off two bends in the farm track by turning sharp left at an old van body and going straight down the field, with the wall close on your left. It regains the farm road at a bridge over the infant river Churnet. Cross the bridge, continue up the farm road and turn left at the T junction, and on past Knowles farm to reach the main road. Turn left along it (there is a grass verge) for 200 yards and fork right into the loop road where the walk began.

Hen Cloud, the Roaches and Ramshaw Rocks from the Morridge

Alternative routes

There are few alternatives available; the OS map shows other rights of way north of Swainsmoor but they pass through an area which has been used as an army firing range. This is now little used, and if firing is to take place there will be very clear warning; but if you do go this way, do not touch any strange objects.

A safe way to extend this walk by a mile or so is to go on to the road at the Mermaid inn, turn left along it to see Blake Mere (the 'Mermaid Pool') just below the road on the left, and then walk up the little hill

Farm scene, Meerbrook

opposite, Merryton Low, to the trig point to admire the view from the highest point of the Morridge. You will often find amateur radio enthusiasts at work here, and sometimes model aircraft or even hang gliders. Return to the Mermaid and carry on as described for the main walk.

Amenities

There is food at the Mermaid inn. The Rock Inn at Upper Hulme serves lunchtime food at weekends only, but the Three Horseshoes three quarters of a mile down the road towards Leek, and the Winking Man two miles up the Buxton road at Royal Cottage, both have food every lunchtime. So does the Lazy Trout at Meerbrook, and there are several pubs and cafes in Leek and Buxton.

The nearest public toilets are at the Tittesworth Reservoir car park (SJ994603). There is also a small cafe here which is open in the summer.

Walk 16: Morridge and Elkstone

Start: the walk starts at a layby 100 yards east of the junction of two minor roads (SK047606) half a mile east of the Mermaid inn, near the highest point of the Morridge (called Merryton Low and marked by a trig pillar) and about five miles west of Hartington. If this layby is full, park on the verge of the minor of the two roads (the one running north-west). There is more space a bit further up this road, near the hilltop, though this fills up at weekends. Don't block the turning loops just off this road, they are sometimes used by army lorries.

Distance: 4 miles (alternative 4¾ miles).

Public transport: there is no convenient bus service.

The walk starts on the high ridge of the Morridge, drops into a valley and continues to the hamlet of Upper Elkstone with its tiny church. This walk is entirely in Staffordshire, on gritstone. About a mile is on minor roads. It crosses a ridge to another valley and returns past the Gliding Club's field near the Mermaid inn.

Not long ago, one would often see full-size gliders circling in the air currents which blow up the side of the ridge. The gliding club appears to have closed down but you may still see model gliders flown near the trig pillar on Merryton Low and the Mermaid pool. You will sometimes see young soldiers training in this area, but there is no firing and they take care not to obstruct the public. (An area north-west of the Mermaid is occasionally used for firing; all approaches are clearly marked by warning signs).

This route should be satisfactory in all but the wettest weather.

The Walk

Leaving the layby, turn left towards Warslow. Although this is a minor road it is straight and cars travel quite fast, so take care. In half a mile, turn down a farm drive on the right. Strictly speaking the right of way leaves the road at a barn a bit further along, then crosses a valley to join the farm drive; but I have met no objection to following the drive all the way.

16. MORRIDGE AND ELKSTONE

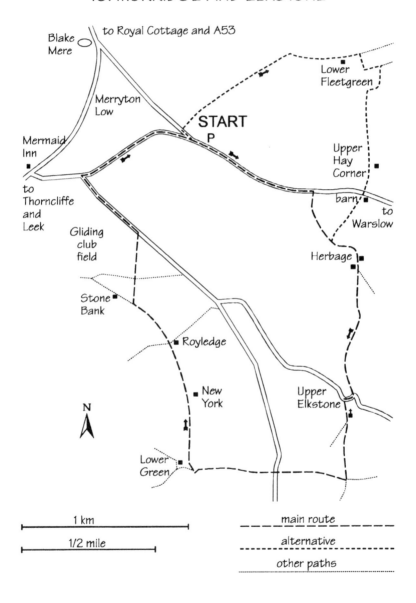

Pass through Herbage farm, and immediately beyond it turn right off the track at a signpost and follow a path down the ridge. Cross the footbridge at the bottom, and bear half-left up the hillside to the few houses of Upper Elkstone village. Turn right along the road and then very shortly left into a lane. Shortly you will pass the church on your left; it is a small square building with a gallery, more like a noncon-formist chapel than a church, and worth a visit.

Continue for a quarter of a mile along the lane past the church. Just before reaching a cottage, cross a stile on your right and climb straight up the hill, crossing another stile and passing a trig pillar. Cross the road by two stiles and continue straight ahead down two fields (or join the farm track to Lower Green farm which runs in the same direction). At the bottom, turn right without crossing the stream. Follow the obvious path parallel to the stream, leaving two farms (New York and Royledge) on your right. A few hundred yards beyond this second farm, a very straight track forks off to the right. Follow this to the road. Turn left along the road to the junction by the gliding field, and then turn right for half a mile to return to your starting point. (The dotted line on the OS map which appears to cut this last corner is not a usable path).

Alternative routes

You can add three quarters of a mile to the walk, but save half a mile of road walking at the cost of another descent and ascent, by going to Lower Fleetgreen farm before visiting Herbage and Elkstone. However parts of this route are rough going, and you should not attempt it after wet weather.

This alternative route starts about a hundred yards up the minor road which branches north-westward off the Warslow – Mermaid road just west of your starting point. There should be a footpath signpost at the start of the path, but at my last visit there was only the hole where it used to stand. So go to the highest point of the embankment, a few yards short of two small trees; and look for a slight ditch, with a low bank marked by some bilberry bushes, running away from the road to the right (north-east). This is the start of the path, though you may have to make a short detour to cross a wet ditch.

The first part of the path is likely to be wet in places so you may have to detour slightly to the left, though walking through the tussocky grass and heather is not easy. Do not be led astray by a sheep track going off to the left. Soon the ditch turns into a little valley with the path, now more easily visible, running along its left lip, and then up onto the crest

Walking down the dale

of the ridge which slopes gently downhill. Where the heather ends you will find a wooden gate in a wire fence, with a stile just to the left.

Cross the stile and walk along either side of the straight ditch which lines up with it until the ditch branches, then go straight ahead along the grassy ridge. Beyond its crest you will see a farm (Lower Fleetgreen) ahead, and this is your objective. First however you have to follow the very faint path down into a narrow valley. Look for a path which slopes up the other side and aim for the point where this meets the bottom of the valley. There is no bridge over the stream, so you will have to jump it as best you can; this should be possible except after much rain.

Now climb the path up the hillside, and when the farm comes in sight again, aim just left of it. You will come to a stile, and beyond it to the farm. The right of way goes just right of the barn and then left through a gate and through the very cluttered farmyard, though you may find a better way through the gate just to the left of the farm.

Either way, join the farm access track and follow it round two bends. About fifty yards beyond the second, turn right along a clear farm track. This descends into a steep valley and crosses a low bridge, by a footpath sign near a redundant footbridge. Now leave the farm track and take a path, muddy at first, which goes up a side valley with a stream on your left (in the direction pointed by the signpost). It crosses a smaller side valley and climbs gradually up the bank on your right to come to the grassy top of the ridge. Now go straight up the ridge, parallel to the electricity poles, aiming for a farmhouse (Upper Hay Corner).

The path leads through two stiles in derelict walls and then just to the right of the farm, to a squeezer stile which is prominent on the skyline. Beyond this, go straight on across a narrow uneven field to meet the road opposite a barn.

Cross the stile just to the right of the barn (FP sign) and bear slightly right, with the wall on your left, to the valley bottom, and then follow the contours round to your left till you reach the farm road near Herbage farm. Turn left along it towards the farm; you are now back on the main route.

Amenities

If you turn right along the road from your starting point, and keep left at the road junction, you will reach the Mermaid inn in about half a mile. If you turn left, you will come to the Greyhound inn at Warslow in two and a half miles. Or turn right from the starting point, fork right at the road junction, bear right near the trig pillar and go on for about two miles, turning left at a T junction. You will reach the A53 at a crossroads by houses; turning right here will bring you immediately to the Winking Man.

There are various inns and cafes in Leek and Hartington. The nearest public toilets are about three miles off at the village hall in Warslow, on the main road opposite the church.

Walk 17: Hulme End and Revidge

Start: the car park (SK103593) at the north end of the Manifold Way at Hulme End, on the B5054 road a couple of miles west of Hartington. This car park is rarely full. It is also possible to park in Warslow village (SK087587), on the straight minor road past the Greyhound Inn (or in its car park if you intend to eat there) or by the village hall opposite the church.

Distance: 4½ miles (alternatives 3 to 5½ miles).

Public transport: there are several buses a day (except Sunday) from Buxton to Hartington via Longnor, Warslow and Hulme End, and occasional buses from Leek to Warslow: on Saturdays these run through from Hanley. There is no Sunday service in winter, other than a single bus from Derby and Ashbourne via Hulme End and Hartington to Buxton and Castleton, returning five or six hours later. There are several buses on this route on summer Sundays and bank holidays; also a ramblers' bus from Mansfield and Derby and, on alternate Sundays, one from Macclesfield.

From the Manifold valley the walk climbs the hillside to Warslow, with a fine view down the valley and across to Ecton hill. A path leads to the summit of the heather moor of Revidge, then down through farmland to cross the B5053 road near Warslow Hall and return across the fields to Hulme End.

The walk is entirely in Staffordshire. The moor at Revidge is on gritstone and the Manifold Way at Hulme End is on limestone, with a band of shale between (hence the hedges). There are one or two wet patches but the walk is reasonable after rain. The heather on Revidge will be at its best in late summer.

There is about half a mile of road walking; most of it has a footway alongside.

The Walk

From the Hulme End car park walk away from the road along the tarmac Manifold Way. This is the route of the former Manifold Light Railway; it closed in the 1930s and the County Council took over the route and

17. HULME END AND REVIDGE

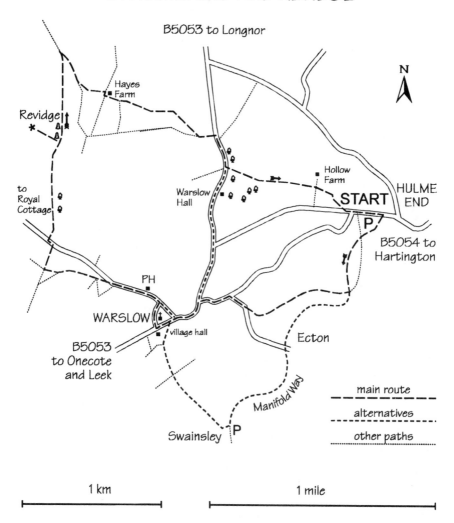

B5053 to Longnor

N

Hayes Farm

Revidge

to Royal Cottage

Hollow Farm

Warslow Hall

START

HULME END

B5054 to Hartington

PH

WARSLOW

village hall

B5053 to Onecote and Leek

Ecton

Manifold Way

Swainsley P

	main route
	alternatives
	other paths

1 km

1 mile

turned it into a path for walkers and cyclists, a real pioneering effort in those days.

In about 600 yards you will see a wicket gate up the bank on your right. Go through it, bear right uphill to a footpath sign, then left keeping between the top of a steep slope and a wall on your right. As you climb the hill, fine views of Ecton Hill and the Manifold valley open up. After about half a mile the path drops past a disused quarry and joins a minor road at a muddy gateway. Turn right up the road, left at the junction, and left again into Warslow village when you reach the main road (which has a footway alongside).

At the next junction you can turn up the very straight road on the right, past the Greyhound inn; but to see more of the village go ahead a little further and turn right past the church, then left when you come out on the straight road near the inn. Continue up the road until it bends right at the end of the village, and go straight ahead along a firm track. Beyond a house the track becomes muddier and in a further 200 yards it bends left. A short way past the bend, a wooden stile is hidden in the hedge on the right. Cross it, then bear left (continuing the original direction of the lane) to another wooden stile and straight on to a stone one. Cross this and turn right, alongside the wall, to reach the road. (You could have saved 200 yards by coming straight along the road to here, but at this point it has no footway).

Tun left for a few yards and then through a stile on the right just beyond a cross-wall (the footpath sign here was mutilated when I last saw it). Walk uphill alongside the wall until the far side of the field comes into view, then bear slightly left to a gate and stile at the left side of a semi-derelict wood. Follow the green track through the wood, with the wall on your left, and onwards past the next gate (there is a stile hidden away on your left) with a wire fence now on your right.

At a log barrier by a small grove of pines the path becomes a firm track. Make a short diversion along a path on your left to the trig pillar (1312 feet, or a neat 400 metres) at the highest point of Revidge, a heather-covered sweep of moorland. In spite of the modest height there is a good view from here, but to see the moor at its best you should come when the heather is in bloom. Return to the track and continue along it, past clumps of stunted pines, for a quarter mile till it meets another track. Turn sharp right along this and follow it, bearing left at a junction, to Hayes farm; a couple of signposts confirm the way.

At the farm go through a gate on the right (signposted) and then left down the field to a stile by another gate, and down the track (past yet another footpath sign) to the next gate, beyond which the path leads across a rushy field. Cross this (not as wet as it looks), bearing rather to the right, until you reach a stile with an iron wicket gate in front of it. Cross this too, and continue with the wall on your left. Eventually the path crosses a dry valley and joins a track which leads quickly to the B5053 road.

Turn right for about 200 yards. At the top of the rise is a footpath sign on the right and a gate opposite. Go through the gate on the left of the road, on a short track which leads through a tree belt into a large field. Cross this, aiming slightly right straight towards Hulme End (where you can now see the green sheds of the former railway terminus), but not quite as far right as the tongue of woodland behind Warslow Hall. Cross a stile by a gate. Carry on along the top of the slope, almost parallel to the road which you can now see on your right. Pass through a muddy gateway and on to a gap in the hedge, which takes you into a field crossed by a farm drive.

You can turn right along the farm drive to the road and left along it to the car park, but if the weather has not been wet it will be more pleasant to go straight ahead, aiming for a large farmhouse where the path joins the road. Turn left along the road, and you will reach the car park in a few hundred yards.

Lime Kilns between Hulme End and Warslow

Alternative routes

If you start from Warslow rather than Hulme End, you can shorten the walk to about three miles at the cost of more road walking. When you reach the B5053 road after walking from Hayes farm, continue to the right along it and ignore the footpath. You will be back at Warslow in less than a mile.

For an extra mile, after leaving the car park stay on the Manifold Way for about a mile and a half until it goes through a gate into another car park at Swainsley. Then cross a stile on the right, half hidden by bushes, about 50 yards beyond the gate. Take the path half-right up the hillside to a stone post, and through a stile on the left, and then go right alongside the hedge. Keep the hedge on your right and cross another stile. Then pass just right of a ruined building, and continue up a thistly field to the gateway which is in a dip at the far end. Go straight on with the fence and streamlet on your left, through another gateway, and through one more gate onto a lane. Turn right along this to reach the main road. Turn right along the main road, then left up a straight road past the Greyhound inn, and you are back on the main route.

Amenities

The Greyhound inn at Warslow is one of my favourites; it serves good food accompanied (when I was last there) by Vivaldi instead of muzak. At Hulme End, just past the bridge in the Hartington direction, is the Manifold Valley Hotel (formerly the Light Railway Hotel); this gets crowded at weekends, and may be a bit up-market for the walker. There are also several inns and cafes in Hartington and Longnor.

There are public toilets in Warslow (at the village hall opposite the church), Longnor and Hartington, but not at Hulme End.

Walk 18: Around Ecton Hill

Start: the small car park on the Manifold Way at the north end of Swainsley tunnel, where the section open to motors ends (SJ091579). This is just off the byroad from Butterton to Ecton and Hulme End. Bird-lovers will enjoy this car park.

Alternatively you can park at the Wetton Mill car park (SJ095561), a mile south along the Manifold Way (this section, including the tunnel, is open to motors); the car park is at the intersection of the Manifold Way with the steep narrow lane from Butterton to Wetton. Or you can park on a wide verge beside the road either side of Ecton (SJ100587 or SJ095581). All these are on or very near the route of the walk. Motorists who prefer to avoid narrow lanes can use the Hulme End car park on the B5054 road two miles west of Hartington (SJ103593), and walk along the Manifold Valley track to the route described, but this will add nearly a mile to the length of the walk.

Distance: 4 miles (alternative 4½ miles).

Public transport: there are no buses near to the main route; for buses to Hulme End see walk 17.

The Manifold Valley is less well known than the parallel valley of the Dove, but is nevertheless one of the most attractive areas of the 'White Peak'. Like the Dove, the Manifold rises on Axe Edge south of Buxton and its upper reaches lie in a wide trough in shale and gritstone country. At Ecton it enters the limestone, and follows a winding course through a narrow valley until it runs into the Dove at Ilam. For the lower part of its course, below Wetton Mill, the bed is dry for most of the year, as the river finds an underground course to emerge at springs in Ilam Park. For several miles upstream from Ilam there is no right-of-way in the valley bottom, but from Beeston Tor past Wetton Mill and Ecton to Hulme End the former Manifold Valley Light Railway track has been converted to a tarmac path (the Manifold Way). Part of this is open to motors, replacing the old motor road which is now almost disused and makes excellent walking.

This is a good walk for a day when it is too windy or too misty to enjoy the hilltops. It is good for rainy weather too, as four-fifths of it are on a firm surface and the rest does not usually get too muddy – although there are a couple of muddy patches, so boots would be a good idea if the ground is wet. The walk takes you round the bottom of Ecton Hill, and is relatively level. Much of it is on a very quiet by-road or on the Manifold Way.

The Manifold Way at Swainsley

The Walk

Walk towards the tunnel mouth from your car, then left and over the road bridge (Ecton Bridge, over the Manifold). You can cut off this corner by taking a stile, hidden in the hedge below the car park, and crossing a plank bridge, but this path may be muddy. Turn into the gated road on your right. This used to be the only road down the valley, but is almost deserted now that traffic can use the tunnel and part of the Manifold Way. If you are a geologist you will find interesting stratification at several points on the left of the road. On the right, across the river, is a round dovecote belonging to Swainsley Hall.

In about a mile you will arrive at a gate by Dale Farm. Turn right along the road. You will come shortly to a road bridge. Do not cross it, unless you want to reach Wetton Mill car park or the picnic area beside it – a popular spot in summer. Instead, go left into Wetton Mill farmyard

18. AROUND ECTON HILL

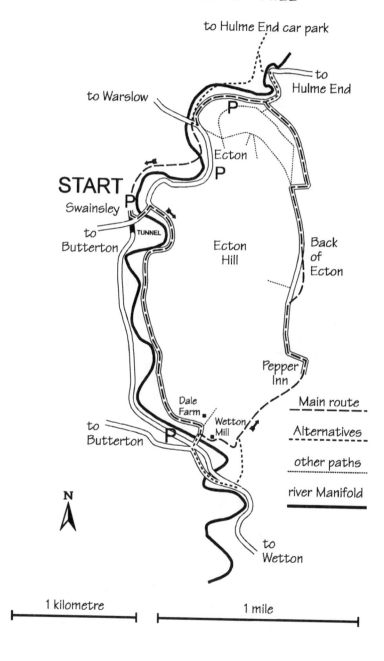

to Hulme End car park

to Hulme End

to Warslow

P

Ecton

P

START

Swainsley

to Butterton

TUNNEL

Ecton Hill

Back of Ecton

Dale Farm

Wetton Mill

to Butterton

P

Pepper Inn

Main route

Alternatives

other paths

river Manifold

N

to Wetton

1 kilometre

1 mile

(there is no longer a mill). There are public toilets here, and a small cafe is often open at weekends.

Do not take the level track through the farmyard but go through a gate immediately to the right of the farmhouse, leaving the rest of the farm buildings on your right. After a short stretch of grass an obvious track slants up the hillside. At the top, turn sharply left (as directed by a blue arrow on a post) and follow the path through a gate and down to the valley bottom. Walk up the valley to your left, alongside a stream which is often dry in its lower reaches. (This is a right of way, though it is not obvious from the OS map). In rather less than a mile you will reach a house, formerly known as Pepper Inn. Go through the gate or the stile beside it, and walk along the metalled road past two right-angle bends. At the next farm you can avoid a short rise in the road by taking a signed footpath which runs almost parallel to the road and rejoins it at the next farm.

In another mile or so you will come to a road junction with a telephone box. Turn left along the road, taking care because this road has a little more traffic than the one you have left. (If you parked at Hulme End turn right instead, then at the second bend cross the river by a footbridge and bear right across a field to rejoin the Manifold valley track, and turn right for the car park. If the field is very wet you may prefer to continue along the road, turning left at each junction to reach the car park).

A short way past the junction, notice obvious remains of copper mining beside the road on your left. Continue for half a mile to a side road on the right, turn down it, then immediately turn left along the Manifold Way. This section is closed to motors, but cyclists can use it and few of them seem to have bells, so walk with care! Shortly the track passes the site of the Ecton creamery, which was one of the reasons for the construction of the Manifold Valley light railway. The creamery closed in the 1930s and the railway very soon after, and its route became one of the first railway lines to be converted to a public path. Up on the hillside you will see the remains of copper mines which were once very prosperous, and also a green-spired house which dates only from the early years of this century after the mines had closed. In three quarters of a mile you will be back at the Swainsley car park.

Alternative route

You can add an interesting half mile to this walk by crossing the bridge at Wetton Mill instead of going into the farmyard. Take the second of two roads to the left (the first is the Manifold Valley track, here used by motors in preference to the older road), using the footbridge by the ford. Walk along the road and over the humped Dafar Bridge. A short way beyond this, in most weather conditions, you will see the river Manifold sink into its bed; the bed remains dry for the next four or five miles, the river re-appearing in the grounds of Ilam Hall (now a country park open to the public).

Where the two roads meet again, go through a gate on the left (behind a small parking space) by a National Trust sign, and walk to your left up the valley. The valley bends to the right where the path from Wetton Mill comes in, and you continue up the valley to Pepper Inn as described for the main walk.

Amenities

Lunchtime food is available at the Black Lion Inn in Butterton, the Royal Oak in Wetton, and the Greyhound in Warslow (one of my favourites) and also at the Manifold Valley Hotel (once the Light Railway Hotel) at Hulme End, though I find this just a bit classy for impecunious hikers. The cafe at Wetton Mill is often open at weekends; there is also a cafe in Wetton village and one at the Manifold Arts Centre in Butterton (on the Grindon road). There are several inns and cafes in Hartington (and also an excellent cheese shop), but the village gets very congested at summer weekends.

There are toilets at Wetton Mill (and in Wetton village and Hartington) but not at the other car parks.

Walk 19: Ecton Hill and Wetton Mill

Start: the walk starts at Ecton (which is a scatter of houses rather than a recognisable village) in the valley of the Manifold, about three miles south-west of Hartington. Park in one of several laybys on the east side of the road (SJ095585), south of the lane leading down from Warslow.

Alternatively use the car park on the Manifold Way at Wetton Mill (095561), but this is approached by narrow lanes. Or use the large car park on the B5054 at Hulme End, about 200 yards west of the bridge (103593), and walk along the Manifold Way to join the route at Ecton; this will make the walk about a mile and a half longer.

Distance: 3 miles (alternative 3½ miles).

Public transport: for buses to Hulme End and Warslow see the description of Walk 17.

This is a short walk but it starts with a steep climb. It offers fine views into the Manifold Valley, and descends into a small quiet dale, before following a disused road up the Manifold valley. It is rather exposed in windy weather, and there is a stretch at Dale Farm which may be muddy after rain (an alternative route is described to avoid this); otherwise it is reasonably firm. About a quarter mile is on a road which carries only light traffic, although it is busier at weekends.

The Walk

From Ecton, walk westwards (downstream) along the road until you can see a house in the valley bottom. Look out for a signposted stile in the wall on your left shortly before you reach the house, and cross it. Follow a grassy path which bears half-right steeply up the hillside.

The path becomes less obvious, but continue up the spur with a fine view down into the Manifold Valley. When you come to a ruined wall, take the path which follows the uphill side of it rather than the more obvious path lower down. The path levels out, and an old hedgebank with hawthorn trees runs up the hill to the left. Follow this, go over the stile at the top, and straight on across the field over the brow of the hill. Pass through a gateway on your right and go diagonally to the far corner

19. ECTON HILL AND WETTON MILL

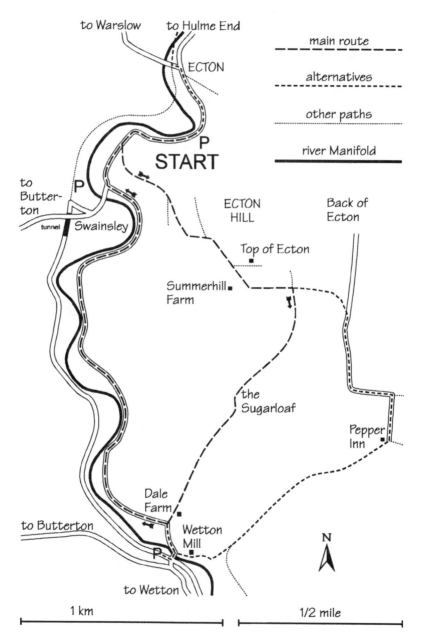

to Warslow   to Hulme End

main route

ECTON

alternatives

other paths

P
START

river Manifold

to
Butter-
ton
P

ECTON
HILL

Back of
Ecton

tunnel Swainsley

Top of Ecton

Summerhill
Farm

the
Sugarloaf

Pepper
Inn

Dale
Farm

to Butterton

Wetton
Mill

N

P

to Wetton

1 km

1/2 mile

of the field, and then on the same heading diagonally across the next field leaving Summerhill Farm (the highest) on your right and Top of Ecton farm well to your left. Go through the gate on your right, and then turn left and follow the wall to reach the farm lane through a gate with a footpath sign.

Turn right, and then immediately cross a stile on your right by another footpath sign, and follow the path down the valley. Just past a National Trust sign the path descends steeply, passing a rocky knob on the left called the 'Sugarloaf'. The dale levels out, and some old logs make this a possible picnic place. Walk down the dale (it can be muddy in places) to Dale Farm, and pass through the farmyard to reach a tarmac lane.

Your way is through the gate on the right, but if you wish you can make a 200 yard detour left to Wetton Mill farm, where there are public toilets and a small cafe which is often open at weekends; the Wetton Mill car park and a picnic site are just across the bridge. Return to Dale Farm and go through the gate, along a tarmac road. This used to be the main road up the valley, but traffic now uses the old railway line (part of the Manifold Way) up this section of the valley, and the old road is disused apart from an occasional farm vehicle. There are some interesting geological exposures in several places on the right of the road, and towards the end of it you can see the round dovecote of Swainsley Hall across the river, with the hall itself set a little further back.

Wetton Mill Farm

The road ends after rather more than a mile at a gate leading onto the main valley road. Turn right, watching out for traffic, and you will pass the stile where you started up the hill and soon after find yourself back at your car.

Alternative routes

You can extend the walk by half a mile if you go by Pepper Inn instead of the Sugarloaf; this may be preferable after heavy rain as it avoids the farmyard at Dale Farm and the muddy section of dale just above it, at the cost of an extra half mile. For this route, when you reach the lane near Top of Ecton farm you should go straight ahead up the lane instead of taking the footpath on the right. At a T junction beyond the crest of the hill, turn right and follow the metalled road to its end at a house which was once the 'Pepper Inn'. Go through the stile by the gate below this house, and walk half a mile down the valley until it swings to the left. Here you will find a path sloping up the valley side to your right. Take this, and a short way beyond a wicket gate the path turns sharp right to descend to the buildings of Wetton Mill. Pass between them; do not go over the bridge but turn right along the lane. This brings you to Dale Farm in about 200 yards. Do not go through the farmyard, but go through the gate on the left and follow the old road up the valley as described for the main walk.

Amenities

As for Walk 18.

Walk 20: Wetton Hill and Thor's Cave

Start: the small car park at Redhurst Crossing in the Manifold Valley (SK099557); or the Wetton Mill car park (SK095561) a quarter of a mile further north along the road if the other is full. The roads to these places from all directions are narrow, and may be congested at summer weekends.

Alternatively you can use the car park in Wetton village (SK109552), which is more easily reached except from the west. This will make the walk a quarter of a mile longer.

Distance: 3½ miles (alternative 4½ miles).

Public transport: there is a very limited bus service to Wetton from Ashbourne; three buses on Saturday and one or two on Thursday.

This walk takes you from the Manifold up a side valley and over Wetton Hill. The hill is pathless but easy walking, and the land belongs to the National Trust. The route descends to Wetton village and then to Thor's Cave, and back to the Manifold Valley.

The walk is entirely in Staffordshire, and on limestone, as will be apparent from the scenery. There is very little road walking, and the route should be reasonable even after rain.

The Walk

Go through the gate at the back of the Redhurst Crossing car park, and turn left to follow the path up the dale for a mile. (If you parked at Wetton Mill you can take a short cut through the farmyard, passing immediately to the right of the house: when the track reaches the top of the ridge, turn sharp left and through a gate to join the path in the dale bottom). The dale is dry at first but a stream appears later. When you reach a building (the former Pepper Inn, now a private house) go through a stile beside the gate to come out on a tarmac lane. Go up this for a few yards; where it turns left, cross a stile on the right and go down the field to cross a footbridge.

Two paths lead from here, one half-left and one half-right. The

20. WETTON HILL AND THOR'S CAVE

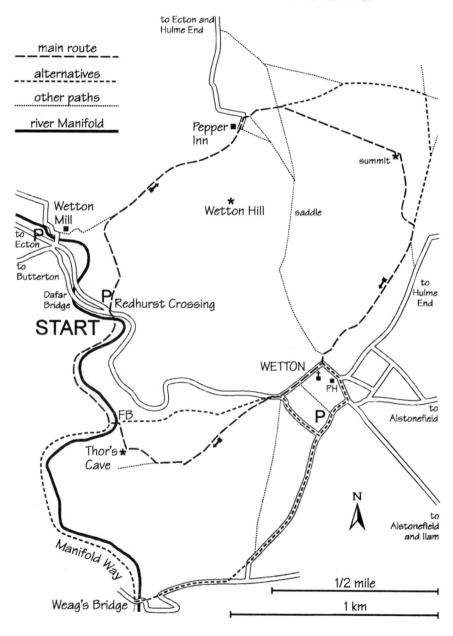

main route

alternatives

other paths

river Manifold

to Ecton and
Hulme End

Pepper ■
Inn

summit ✳

Wetton
Mill

✳
Wetton Hill

saddle

to
Ecton

P

to
Butterton

Dafar
Bridge

P Redhurst Crossing

to
Hulme
End

START

WETTON

PH

FB

P

to
Alstonefield

Thor's ✳
Cave

N
Λ

to
Alstonefield
and Ilam

Manifold Way

Weag's Bridge

1/2 mile

1 km

right-hand one goes between two hills; the map names the right-hand hill as Wetton Hill but does not name the other, higher, one. Both are on National Trust land and there seems to be no objection to walkers leaving the right of way. Our route goes up the larger hill. So follow the left-hand path across the hillside towards a stone post. Just before reaching it, you cross another path which leads up to the saddle.

Beyond the stone post the path contours round the hillside. Leave it and head straight up the hill to the summit, and admire the view while you get your breath back. (If you want to avoid the climb, or prefer to stick to the right of way, follow the path as it contours round the hill. Where the path comes to a stile, do not cross it but continue round the foot of the hill).

The far side of the hill is too steep to descend directly, so bear to the right. When you near a wall corner the slope eases, and you can head left down a little valley past a capped mineshaft to regain the path which runs round the hill. Below you a stretch of the road comes straight towards the hill and then turns away; almost in line with this you will find a wooden stile, which you should cross.

Now turn right and you will see two stiles in the next wall. Take the one on the right, which is both a stone squeezer and a wooden step stile, and continue in the same line through several more stiles. When you find a wall on your right, continue alongside it through more stiles. Eventually a stone step stile brings you into a yard in front of a house. Pass in front of the house into a lane which quickly brings you to a bend in the road in Wetton Village.

The village is built around roads which form a large square. The direct route is the right-hand road, past the church and a tea-shop, to the next junction where your road bears slightly to the right. However if you want to visit the inn, car park, or toilets, take the left-hand road; turn right after the Royal Oak, and you will come to the car park and toilets in about 200 yards. Continue in the same direction, turn right at the junction and left at the next one, and you are back on the main route.

A few yards beyond the junction, a walled track diverges on the left. In the angle between this and the road, a footpath runs down to the lowest point in the field. You can save a couple of hundred yards and some steep sections by taking this path, which brings you to the footbridge over the Manifold. However that way misses out Thor's cave. So take the walled track, which is signposted 'Concessionary footpath to Thor's Cave'. About half a mile along this track, beyond a gate, a sign directs you over a stone step-stile on your right. Once over this turn left down the hill, past a broken fence, and take the obvious path which dips and then rises slightly to a wooden stile.

Cross the stile. You can make a short excursion straight ahead to the hilltop for the sake of the view, but your route is the path leading down the hillside to your right. This soon brings you to Thor's cave, a vast arch in the hillside with a short cave within. You can explore, but be careful; the rock is slippery. Prehistoric remains were found in the cave, but of course there is nothing of them to see now. What you can see is a magnificent view up the Manifold valley far below you. It is a popular spot; you are unlikely to have it to yourself.

Thor's Cave

A steep well-trodden footpath leads down to a footbridge, joining the shorter route on the way. You will probably find that the river is dry. In all but the wettest weather it disappears underground near Dafar Bridge, a short way upstream from your starting point, and returns to the surface several miles downstream close to Ilam Hall. Cross the bridge and turn right along the Manifold Way. Motor vehicles are not allowed to use this section of the way, but it is popular with cyclists and you can rarely hear them coming up behind you – you have been warned! Half a mile along this path will bring you back to your starting point at Redhurst crossing.

If you parked at Wetton Mill you have a choice of two roads from here, since this section of the Manifold Way is open to cars; the old road on the left, over the hump-backed Dafar Bridge, is therefore more

Manifold Way near Redhurst Crossing

pleasant walking. Look out (except after wet weather) for the Manifold sinking into its bed just before you reach the bridge. The road goes through a shallow ford just before the Wetton Mill car park, but there is a footbridge.

Alternative routes

You can add an extra mile to your walk if you extend it to Weag's Bridge. This will mean missing out Thor's Cave, though you can scramble up to it and back from the valley footpath if you have that much energy left over.

To take this extended route, when you reach Wetton turn left past the Royal Oak and right past the car park, but go straight on at the next junction instead of turning left. In half a mile, shortly after the lane bends left and becomes steeper, go through a stile on the right. Walk straight down the hill, with a wall on your right, to rejoin the road and turn right along it. (If you miss the stile at the top, just go on down the road and turn right at the junction). Follow the road down to the valley; where it turns very sharply left you can cut off a corner by walking straight ahead to rejoin the road at a lower bend.

At the valley bottom, cross Weag's Bridge and turn right along the

Approaching Thor's Cave

Manifold Way, which forms a car park for a few yards before it returns to being a footpath and cycle way. It is now just over a mile back to Redhurst Crossing where the walk began. You will pass a concrete footbridge on your right; cross it and climb the hill if you want to visit Thor's Cave, returning to the valley bottom by the same path.

Amenities

The Royal Oak in Wetton and the Black Lion in Butterton both provide lunchtime food. There is a tearoom in Wetton, on the route of the walk near the point where you leave the village, and a small cafe at Wetton Mill, a quarter mile up the valley from your starting point, which is often open at weekends. In summer you may find an ice cream van near the car park where the walk starts.

There are public toilets near the route at the car park in Wetton village, and in the valley at Wetton Mill (at the farm, across the bridge from the car park).

Walk 21: Wetton and Bincliff

Start: the car park (SK109552) in the quiet village of Wetton, between the Dove and Manifold valleys. There is no other practical parking place, except in the Manifold Valley at Weag's Bridge, and this would add about a mile and a stiff climb to the walk; it is impossible to park in any of the narrow lanes between Wetton and Bincliff.

Distance: 3 miles (alternative 4½ miles).

Public transport: there is a very sparse bus service from Ashbourne to Wetton, via Alstonefield, on Thursdays and Saturdays only.

Two miles of the lower Manifold Valley, from the point where it is joined by the river Hamps (and the Manifold Way) down to Rushley Bridge above Ilam, are forbidden territory – there is no right of way along the valley bottom. But a footpath running along the rim of the valley, past abandoned lead mines at Bincliff, gives a fine view down into this stretch of the valley and back upstream as far as Beeston Tor. The walk can be extended along the valley side to Castern Hall.

This walk is entirely within Staffordshire, and on limestone. For much of the year this stretch of the Manifold is dry; the Manifold and the Hamps both sink into their beds further upstream, and the water re-appears at springs close to Ilam Hall.

A short part of this route may be muddy after heavy rain, although not impassable. There is very little road walking.

The Walk

From the car park, walk left along the road for a hundred yards or so to a gateway on your right, through which a gravel track runs up a narrow field to a small caravan site. Strictly speaking you should pass the gateway and go through a squeezer stile set a little back from the road by a footpath sign, then cross the track and the field diagonally to another squeezer stile. Continue diagonally across several more fields, aiming for a barn and tree on the skyline. Just before you reach the barn there is a wall corner on your left, and a step stile in the wall facing you

21. WETTON AND BINCLIFF

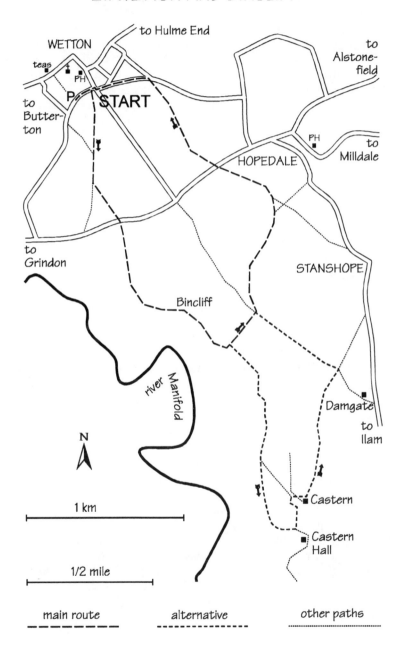

to Hulme End

WETTON

teas

PH

to Butter-ton

P START

to Alstone-field

PH

to Milldale

HOPEDALE

to Grindon

STANSHOPE

Bincliff

river Manifold

N

Damgate

to Ilam

Castern

1 km

Castern Hall

1/2 mile

main route

alternative

other paths

a few yards from the corner. Cross this and go down the field with the wall on your right.

Cross the road by a pair of squeezer stiles, and go straight across the field past an old dewpond and through another squeezer stile. (If the field is very muddy, make a short detour along the road to the left). Now bear right along the obvious path along the contour. Where this fades, look for a squeezer stile between a hawthorn tree and a drinking trough set in the wall. Go through the stile and straight on, climbing slightly. You will see evidence of old lead mines on the left, and on the right you have a fine view down into the pathless stretch of the Manifold Valley. Looking upstream you have also a good view of the cliff called Beeston Tor on the near side of the valley, and of the Hamps valley which joins the Manifold opposite Beeston Tor.

After walking for half a mile along the rim of the valley you will cross a wooden stile, and just beyond it is a group of signs telling you that the path ahead is a dead end, giving access only to a nature reserve (which you can visit). So go over a stile on your left. Beyond this, an extension of the walk (indicated by a sign) goes through a gate on the right for Castern; but the main walk goes straight ahead along a track to the left of mine spoil heaps. It shortly comes to an unmetalled lane by a very tall iron footpath signpost. (The extended route rejoins here).

The lane to the left leads straight back to Wetton; but for a more pleasant and only slightly longer path, go through the squeezer stile opposite and half-left across the field to another squeezer. Through this, go down the valley through a gateway and two more squeezers, always keeping the wall close on your left. Where this wall swings away to the left, go half-left through a gateway and continue with a wall on your right. (Officially the right of way crosses this wall by a stile just right of the gate, and then goes along the other side of it for a few yards to cross back by another stile; do this if you cannot open the gate).

Beyond the next gateway go half-left across the field, making for the top end of a row of trees and crossing another squeezer on the way. By the trees you will find a narrow road, which you cross by two more squeezers (with footpath signs). Climb the slope and cross a wooden stile. Now bear half-left again. Beyond another squeezer, aim just left of the corner of a broken wall with bushes by it. Turn half-right at the corner to follow the wall-cum-hedge on your right, and cross two squeezers close together. Now go straight on to cross a squeezer by a small tree – aim just left of the conical hill on the skyline – and then on across another squeezer. You can now see a stretch of narrow road ahead. Aim for this, and you will reach a last squeezer giving onto the road – be careful of the barbed wire. Turn left along the road into the village. Ignore the first road on the right; at the T junction, turn right and then immediately left to return to the car park (or straight on for the Royal Oak, which you can see from here).

Stile near Damgate

Alternative route

The walk can easily be extended to Castern, adding another mile and a half. It continues along the edge of the Manifold valley, although set back from it so the view is less extensive, to Castern farm; a few extra yards let you look at the 18th century Castern Hall (a private house).

After crossing the stile from the valley-rim footpath at Bincliff, instead of going straight ahead on the track you should turn right through a gate – there is a notice to indicate the way towards Ilam. The path crosses the field, dropping slightly and going just left of a grassy mound, and leads through a squeezer stile alongside a gate in the far corner. Beyond this the path curves round the head of a small side valley, losing height and becoming a clear green track, and goes through a stile by a gate just in front of a tree. (You can take a short cut from here, by bearing slightly left up the hillside to cross a stile and come out at a signpost above Castern Farm; but the path is not obvious on the ground, although it is a right of way). The track then continues, more or less level, through several fields keeping close to a wall on your right.

Eventually Castern Hall comes in sight and you reach a gate, with a stile each side, in a wire fence. Beyond this you come to a tarmac farm road. Turn left along it (away from the Hall – though you can make a short detour to look at it first) towards Castern Farm; but just beyond a house, go through a signposted stile on the left and straight up the field to cross a squeezer stile on the skyline.

Turn right alongside the wall to a footpath sign (this is where the short cut comes out), through the gate beside it, and right down the concrete track towards the farm for a few yards. Beyond the first shed, go left of the farm buildings to a pair of gates. Cross the iron stile beyond the second gate. There is a footpath sign here; go in the direction it points, uphill and rather to the right, and you will see a gate in the wall which runs up the dry valley on your right. Cross the stile near the gate and turn left up the valley, alongside the wall. Stay alongside this wall through several waymarked stiles (the next but one is hard to see until you are near it). Beyond the crest of the ridge you will come to a four-way footpath signpost, with a stile ahead. Do not cross it, but go through the narrow iron gate on your left (signposted to Wetton) and across several fields, keeping close to the wall on your right. Eventually the path becomes a walled track and you soon come to the tall iron signpost mentioned in the description of the main route. Cross the stile on your right to continue along the main route, or go ahead along the lane for the shortest way back to Wetton.

Amenities

The Royal Oak in Wetton provides hot food at lunchtime, and there is also a tea-room in the village, on the road which passes the church; from the car park turn right and right again, or take the footpath which runs from the car park across to this road. In Alstonefield, a mile and a half east, there is food at the George inn and a tea-room at the post office. To the north there is the Manifold Valley Hotel at Hulme End. The Watts Russell Arms at Hopedale, just off the road from Alstonefield to Wetton and Ilam, also offers food although I have not tried it.

There are public toilets at the car park in Wetton.

Walk 22: Throwley Hall and Soles Hollow

Start: the car park at Weag's Bridge (SK100542) in the Manifold Valley, on the minor road from Grindon to Wetton and Alstonefield. This road is winding, steep and narrow in places so take particular care – at busy weekends you may need to reverse to passing places. You can save about half a mile of walking if you park in the camp site at Beeston Tor farm, but there is a small charge for this (pay at the farm).

The only other safe parking is at the car parks in Grindon and Wetton villages, but either of these will add a mile and a half to your walk.

Distance: 4 miles (alternatives $3\frac{1}{2}$ to 5 miles).

Public transport: there is no bus close to the route. Wetton has very occasional buses on Thursday and Saturday, and Grindon on Wednesday and Saturday.

There are five buses a day (including Sunday) on the Derby – Ashbourne – Leek – Manchester route; these pass the southern end of the Manifold Way at Waterhouses on the A523, about a mile from Lee House and a little further (via Calton) from Slade House.

The walk takes you from the Manifold Valley at Weag's Bridge up to Throwley Hall, a handsome farmhouse with the ruins of its Elizabethan predecessor nearby; then past Slade House and down to the Manifold Way in the Hamps valley by way of Soles Hollow. There are good views into that part of the Manifold Valley, between Beeston Tor and Rushley Bridge, which has no footpath.

The walk is entirely in Staffordshire, and on limestone. Most of it is satisfactory underfoot but the meadow near Throwley Hall can be wet, and part of the path down Soles Hollow slippery, in wet weather. There is very little road walking. There are two fairly long, though reasonably gentle, ascents.

The Walk

Go back to the car park entrance. Across the road you will see two tarmac tracks which run parallel. Take the left-hand one (the other, with a gate and 'no cars' sign, is the Manifold Way by which you will return). Through the vegetation on your left you will see the bed of the river Manifold. It is dry for most of the year – the water finds an underground route from Dafar Bridge, further up the valley, to Ilam. The farm track passes through a small camp site and crosses a side stream, the Hamps, which is also usually dry. The wooden shed by the bridge was once a tearoom, serving visitors brought into the valley by the light railway whose route now forms the Manifold Way footpath. On your left you can see the impressive limestone rock face of Beeston Tor, often dotted with climbers.

Beeston Tor

Where the track forks at the entrance to Beeston Tor Farm, take the right fork which leads uphill. It turns into a side valley, passing a stone barn and a derelict iron Dutch barn. Where the valley bottom rises to the level of the track, a gate and stile take you into a field with prominent terraces, presumably the result of medieval farming. The track becomes indistinct in the grass; keep on up the bottom of the valley to the right of the terraces. At the top of the field, bear left for a short way alongside

22. THROWLEY HALL AND SOLES HOLLOW

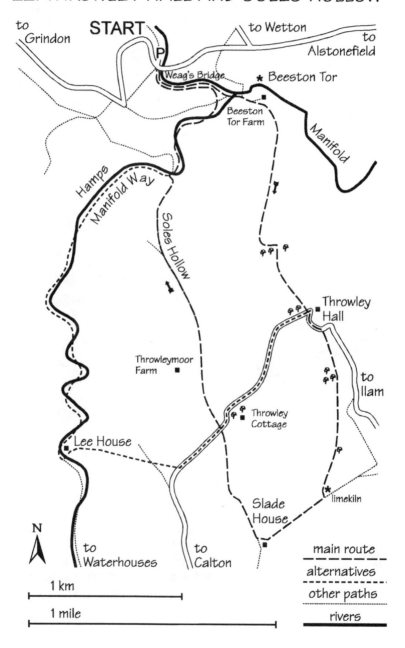

a wall. Where this turns sharply right, go straight on (as indicated by a footpath sign), with another wall and a tree belt shortly on your right. This wall turns right at a heap of rubble; follow it and cross the stile.

From here there is a clear track down the field to Throwley Hall, a big farm which you can see to the left of a clump of trees. The track passes through the farmyard, but this is not the right of way; so aim towards the right-hand end of the farm buildings and you will come to a wooden stile at the left end of a tree belt. Cross this and follow the path through the trees till you meet the end of the farmyard, and turn onto the tarmac byroad.

Throwley Old Hall

Turn left along the road, with farm buildings on your right and the imposing farmhouse on the left. Beyond it are the ruins of an earlier, probably Elizabethan, house. Where the wall on your right ends, leave the road and take a route which diverges to its right, climbing slowly up the hillside; a footpath sign indicates the direction. At first the path is not visible on the ground, but you will shortly see a small walled wood ahead; aim for the left-hand edge of this. As you approach it the path becomes visible. It curves slightly right as it passes the wood, still climbing gently, and aims for an isolated tree.

Cross a ladder stile in the dip just to the right of the tree. Now aim half-left over the flank of the hill, and another ladder stile will come in sight. Cross this and continue in the same direction, aiming for the far corner of the field which is hidden at first. As you come over the rise you will see a couple of scrubby trees and a low stone structure ahead. When you get nearer you will find that this is the top of a well-preserved lime kiln, set in a small depression. Pass either side of it to a signpost at a wall gap in the field corner. Go half-right, along a walled green track, and straight on up the field with a ruined wall and barn on your left.

As you approach Slade House the track turns right, but the right of way goes straight ahead through two waymarked squeezer stiles. Beyond the second the path follows a wall round to another footpath sign at a track junction. Turn right, away from the buildings, along a firm farm road. In half a mile this ends at a gate onto a tarmac byroad.

Go straight ahead, as indicated by a footpath sign, keeping to the lowest part of the valley and leaving Throwleymoor Farm well to your left. The valley (Soles Hollow) deepens; there is no obvious path over the grass but there are stiles, at one of which you cross the wall which runs along the valley bottom. Continue down the valley. Where a track turns up the hillside, keep in the valley bottom. The path is rocky (and slippery in wet weather) for a few hundred yards, but then improves. Eventually it brings you through a wicket gate onto a tarmac footpath. This is the Manifold Way (though here it runs in the valley of the Hamps, a tributary of the Manifold), which follows the route of the old light railway.

Turn right along the Manifold Way, watching out for silent cyclists, and you will be back at the Weag's Bridge car park in about half a mile.

Alternatives

You can shorten the walk by about three quarters of a mile if you leave out Slade House. When you reach the road at Throwley Hall, turn right instead of left along it. In half a mile, just past a wood, the road dips and a footpath signpost directs you to the right, down the valley. Take this and you are back on the main route.

For an extra mile or so, when you reach the byroad and footpath sign at the top of Soles Hollow from Slade House, turn left along the byroad (or continue along it if you came the direct way from Throwley Hall). In about 300 yards, immediately past a cattle grid, cross a stile on the right and head straight down a little side valley. Keep to the valley bottom, ignoring a track which leads round the hillside on the right.

The Manifold Way

You will join the Manifold Way near Lee House (where refreshments are sometimes available). Turn right along this metalled footpath, and follow it for about two miles to the Weag's Bridge car park. Although this shows you more of the Hamps Valley, it has to be said that this is not the most exciting stretch of it.

Amenities

The Cavalier in Grindon and the Royal Oak in Wetton both serve hot food at midday. A little further off are the George in Alstonefield and the Black Lion in Butterton. There are cafes in Wetton, Alstonefield and Butterton.

There are public toilets at the car parks in Wetton and Alstonefield, but the nearest on the west side of the valley are at Warslow village hall and at Waterhouses car park.

Walk 23: Axe Edge and Dove Head

Start: the car park at Cistern's Clough (SK034698), formed by a loop of road which is now bypassed by the A53 Buxton to Leek road about three miles south of Buxton.

Parking in the minor roads followed by part of this walk is difficult, but you can park on the wide grass verge of the A53 either side of Dove Head farm (SK031684).

Distance: 3 Miles (alternative 3½ miles).

Public transport: there are three or four buses a day, weekdays and Sundays, from Hanley and Leek to Buxton (some continuing to Sheffield) and back. They stop at the bus shelter at Cistern's Clough car park.

This walk explores a corner of Axe Edge moor and the highest reaches of the river Dove, around its source in the gritstone country of the western edge of the Park. It can be wet after rain, so is best kept for drier weather – preferably a clear day if you are to see the fine views at their best.

The main walk is entirely in Derbyshire, but the alternative suggested strays into Staffordshire for half a mile or so near Dove Head, which is on the boundary (this follows the Dove for the whole length within the Park of that river). There is about a mile of road walking, along very quiet byroads.

The Walk

Go through the stile at the back of the car park, just to the right of the stream, and walk up the clough to the minor road. The path follows the route of an old tramway which served coal mines on Axe Edge. As you climb, turn round to admire the view over the Dove valley, with Chrome Hill prominent. At the road you are 520 metres (1700 feet) above sea level near the highest point of Axe Edge; this is the watershed between the Dove and Manifold, which run via the Trent and Humber into the North Sea, and the Dane and Goyt which run via the Mersey into the Irish Sea. All four of these rivers rise within a couple of miles of where you are standing.

23. AXE EDGE AND DOVE HEAD

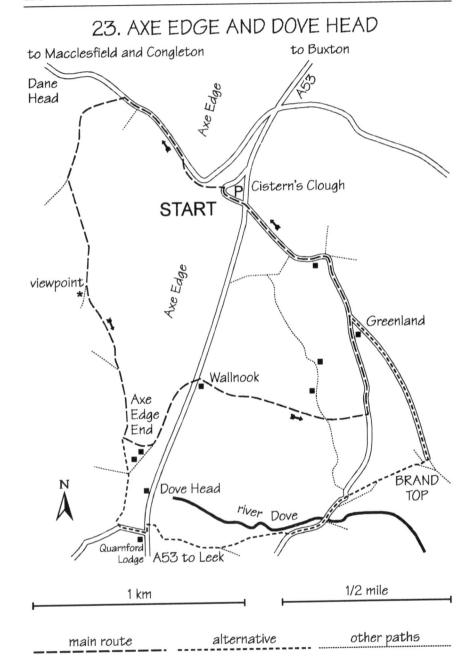

to Macclesfield and Congleton

to Buxton

Dane Head

Axe Edge

A53

P Cistern's Clough

START

viewpoint
*

Axe Edge

Greenland

Wallnook

Axe Edge End

N

BRAND TOP

Dove Head

river Dove

Quarnford Lodge

A53 to Leek

1 km

1/2 mile

main route — — — — alternative ·········· other paths

Follow the road to the left for about a quarter of a mile; ignore the first track (with log barrier) on the left and take the second. (If you continue along the road for a hundred yards you will meet the Dane very close to its source, which is on private land. Return by the road to this point). This path is wet in places, and leads over the lowest part of a shallow saddle. Where a small stream appears on the left and a gate ahead, look out for a faint track forking left and leading across the stream to a small spoil heap and on along the hillside. Take this, and continue for about a quarter of a mile until a group of rocks can be seen on the ridge ahead.

A short way before this, fork left (though you may like to make a detour to the rocks for the sake of the view; on a clear day it extends to the Clwddian Hills in Wales and the Clee hills in Shropshire). As this path approaches a farm track it bears left and joins the track just beyond a gate. Go left along the track, turning left with it when it approaches a wall (the alternative route goes straight on here), and continue with it to the road. Before joining the road there is a fine view to the right over the head of the Dove valley to the sharp-pointed Parkhouse and Chrome Hills, with another limestone hill, High Wheeldon, just to their right. The source of the Dove itself is just beyond the main road a short way to your right, close to Dove Head farm, although the choice of this

Bridge near Dove Head

particular stream from the several which meet near here seems a bit arbitrary – the stream which passes the Cistern's Clough car park has as good a claim.

Cross the road and pass to the left of Wallnook cottage. Go through a wicket gate just behind the cottage, then left to a farm gate and straight down the field with the wall on your right. When you cross a rather high stile you will find walls on both sides. Go on down the hill, over a wet patch at the bottom, and cross a stile onto a farm track. The stream which you cross here is another infant branch of the Dove. Go straight ahead up the hill until you meet a minor road, and turn left along it. Keep left at the next junction, drop to the valley, and continue up a steep hill to the main road. The car park is directly opposite.

Alternative route

If you want to go nearer the actual source of the Dove, after coming off the moor onto a farm track go straight ahead at the bend, through an iron gate, instead of bearing left with the track to the main road. After a short walk along a walled green track you will come onto a tarmac lane. Go straight ahead, then left along a minor road to reach the main road at Quarnford Lodge (a licensed restaurant, but apparently not open at lunchtime). A short way to the left along the main road is Dove Head farm; the Dove rises at a spring in a small wood on the other side of the road, but this is on private land.

Go over the stile (with a footpath sign) almost opposite the lane you came down, and half-right alongside an old wall; then follow the wall on your right downhill. Where it crosses a depression there is an obvious track. Now go down the field to cross a wooden stile in the fence at the bottom, just right of a small tree. From here follow the electricity wires down to the lowest point of the field, keeping close to the stream bank to avoid the worst of the wet patches. At the bottom of the field a stile takes you onto a by-road.

Turn left along this road, over the bridge and up the hill. You could continue along the road, past the end of a track on the left where the main route joins this road, but to add a little more to the walk go straight ahead up a walled track where the road bends left shortly after you join it. If the track is too wet, there is a parallel footpath very close to it on the right. At the top is the hamlet of Brand Top. Turn left along the only metalled road, and in half a mile you will come to a road junction just by a house. Bear right, and you are back on the main route – down the hill and up the long hill opposite to reach the car park.

An inviting stile

If you have the OS 'Outdoor Leisure' map you will see that there is a dense network of rights of way in this area, and you can pick your own route among them. Those I have explored are unobstructed (apart from short deviations round houses) with adequate stiles and footbridges, but some of them are little used and so not clear on the ground, and they can be very muddy after rain.

Amenities

The Traveller's rest, at Flash Bar on the main road about a mile south of Cistern's Clough, may serve food but was closed for refurbishing when I last saw it. However if you continue for a quarter of a mile further along the main road, and then turn right, you will come to the tiny village of Flash ('the highest in England') and you will find food at the New Inn. There are many inns and cafes in Buxton.

The nearest public toilets are at the car park and picnic site at Grin Low, near Buxton (SK047721) or just beyond the traffic lights at Burbage church on the outskirts of Buxton.

Walk 24: Hollinsclough and Chrome Hill

Start: in the tiny village of Hollinsclough, four miles due south of Buxton and best approached via Longnor: all other roads are steep and narrow. Park on the wide verge near the telephone box (SK065665). There is no other practicable parking place on the main route.

Distance: 3¼ miles (alternatives 2½ to 3¾ miles).

Public transport: the bus service to Hollinsclough is very sparse, but there are several buses a day from Buxton to Longnor. These pass over Glutton Bridge, which is about half a mile from the nearest part of the route. From the Buxton side of Glutton Bridge turn westwards, near a telephone box, along a minor road. In half a mile, when the road has become unfenced, take the drive to a house on the left (Stannery) with a cattle grid between prominent gateposts; you are now on the main route of the walk, which will eventually bring you back to this point.

In the upper reaches of the Dove valley the stream runs along the boundary between shale and millstone grit, to the south-west, and reef limestone to the north-east. The reef limestone gives rise to two spectacular craggy hills, Chrome and Parkhurst. The main route includes a scramble along the crest of Chrome Hill. This is one of the most enjoyable walks in the district, on a hill which gives the feeling of a real mountain though of course on a small scale. The route also crosses an old packhorse bridge, with an optional extension to a second.

The walk starts and ends in Staffordshire, but Chrome Hill is in Derbyshire – the river Dove forms the boundary. Short stretches are on very quiet byroads.

The route is passable after rain, though there are a few muddy patches. The crest of Chrome Hill has a steep drop on either side, so it should be avoided in very high winds – an alternative path allows this.

The Walk

From the telephone box at Hollinsclough go straight on across the road

24. HOLLINSCLOUGH AND CHROME HILL

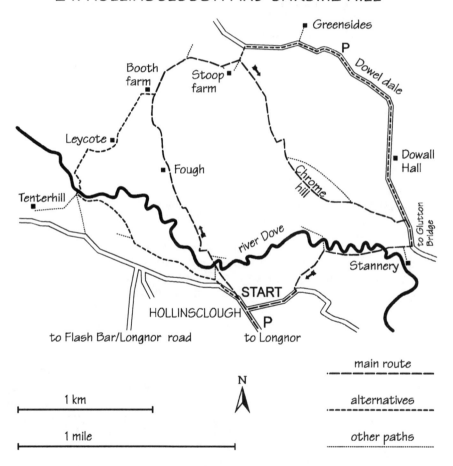

Greensides

P

Dowel dale

Booth farm

Stoop farm

Leycote

Fough

Chrome hill

Dowall Hall

Tenterhill

river Dove

to Glutton Bridge

Stannery

START

HOLLINSCLOUGH

P

to Flash Bar/Longnor road

to Longnor

N

1 km

1 mile

main route

alternatives

other paths

junction, and up the hill past the postbox and a stone water trough. Turn right immediately beyond a barn, through a gate with the remains of a squeezer stile alongside, and then left through a gate, to go gently downhill alongside a wall on your right. This will bring you to a stone packhorse bridge – notice how low the parapet is, to avoid catching on the horses' loads.

Go over the bridge and up the cobbled path ahead, which brings you to a farm track; turn left along it. (A path to the left just past the bridge cuts off a corner, but is often muddy). Follow the farm track up the side of the valley for about a mile. Where you pass an isolated house (Fough) the track becomes firmer underfoot. It levels out, and you pass Booth Farm a short way off on your left. Your track joins the tarmac farm road; continue right along it for two hundred yards to where another track turns off to the right, towards Stoop Farm which you can see below a belt of trees. Take this track, but do not follow it to the farm; instead, branch off to the left to pass behind the trees, through two stiles, and then half-left up the field to join the farm track at a gateway with a cattle grid and footpath sign.

Do not cross the cattle grid, but cross the track and go over the stile marked 'Concessionary path to Glutton Bridge via Chrome Hill'. This path is clearly waymarked, so you will only need the following directions if some of the marks have gone astray. Go straight on over two stiles, keeping the wall on your left, and on to a waymark post in a wall gap. Here turn half-right down the field, with a wire fence to your left and a gully on the right. In wet weather you will see a stream run down the gully to disappear into loose rocks in a large swallowhole, surrounded by limestone crags.

Continue down the slope, and cross a stile on the left a short way above a ruined barn. The path slopes gently downhill, and then beyond another stile turns sharp left for a short but steep pull up a grassy slope to the ridge, where it turns right alongside a wall. Now the waymarked path bears right to the summit of the ridge, and you have an exhilarating easy scramble over the series of rocky knolls which form the summit of Chrome Hill, eventually descending the end of the ridge beyond the last and highest of them. Watch out for a cave and a natural arch in the rock on your left.

If you want a less energetic or exposed route, you can carry on along the wall instead of the top of the ridge. However, even this is not uneventful because you will reach a point where the wall ends at the top of a steep crag. From here you must take either of the narrow tracks which continue level across the steep hillside. Although these are not difficult, you need to take care at a few rocky stretches. At last these paths bring you out on the path descending the end of the ridge from the summit.

Go down the grassy slope to a step-stile by a tree, and on along the lower ridge beyond, heading straight towards the conical Parkhouse Hill on the other side of the byroad. Where you approach the end of this ridge the waymarks bear right, and then left to a stile just to the right of the cattle grid.

Turn right along the road for 200 yards, with Parkhouse Hill on your left. Turn down the drive on the right which goes to an isolated house called Stannery. (If you want the bus stop at Glutton Bridge, go straight on along the road instead). Just beyond the gateposts, where the drive turns left, you should go straight on along a fainter track by a wooden post. The track soon becomes clearer and muddier, and crosses the Dove by a ford and a concrete footbridge. Go straight on along the track. It becomes firmer, and joins another tarmac farm track. Turn left along this to the road, and then right into Hollinsclough village. Passing the ornate old school building (dated 1840) on your right you will soon be back at your car.

Chrome Hill

Alternative route

The scramble over Chrome Hill, or alongside it, is fairly strenuous, and may not be safe for small children. It can be avoided, without adding much to the distance, by using the quiet road down Dowel Dale. To do this, after passing behind Stoop Farm do not take the concessionary path, but turn left over the cattle grid and follow the farm road for a short way till it meets a byroad. Turn right along this, down the hill, past Greenside farm and down Dowel Dale.

Before and around Greenside you will see many swallow holes, where in wet weather streams run down the slope to disappear in the loose rocks at the bottom, running underground to re-appear further down the valley. Beyond this farm and the cattle grid, on the left, is a large pothole in the rock, the Owl Hole; but this has recently been fenced off and is now hard to see. It is, alas, half full of rubbish.

The dry dale below the farm is Dowel Dale. It bends right, and then emerges suddenly into a more open landscape at Dowall Hall farm. A few yards to the right of the road, opposite the farm entrance, is a narrow cave from which a stream emerges (except in very dry weather); presumably this is the water that went into the swallow holes above the dale. Continue along the road and over the cattle grid, where you rejoin the main route below Parkhouse Hill.

Another alternative route adds about half a mile to the distance and takes in another very attractive packhorse bridge, but is likely to be wet in parts after rain. Leave Hollinsclough as described for the main route, but continue past the barn up the hill for a hundred yards to a bridle way sign and go through the small iron gate on the right. Beyond a short stony stretch the wall on your right ends and the path divides. Take the green path to the left, which runs slightly uphill on a pronounced terrace. At a broken wall the path forks; take the left fork.

Beyond a wooden stile among trees the path divides to cross a wet patch; the lowest branch has stepping stones. The path is clear, climbing gently with a wall on the left and then crossing to the right of the wall. Where a green track goes steeply up the hill, do not take it but go towards a ruinous barn and continue along the path.

At a fork, a waymark post indicates the lower track. However this soon comes to a very wet patch and you may need to go well to the left, just above the trees, to cross it. The path is clear, but when it descends towards the stream there is a flat wet area which can be skirted to the left.

Step over a narrow side stream, over a wooden stile, and by stepping stones over another side stream, and then cross an elegant stone packhorse bridge on a track which descends from Tenterhill farm. Follow the stony sunken packhorse road which winds steeply up the hillside. In the steepest places, many of the old stone setts remain. The path levels out, and then dips slightly to farm buildings at Leycote. Turn left in front of the house and follow a gravel track to Booth Farm, where you bear right in front of the houses on a tarmac farm road which passes through two gates. (The main route, via Fough, joins just after the second). Look out for the Stoop Farm junction on the right about two hundred yards beyond the second gate, and follow the instructions for the main route.

If you want a shorter walk which still includes Chrome Hill, take the very minor road through Dowel Dale. Park at the top of the dale, about a hundred yards below the cattle grid near Greenside farm where the road ceases to be unfenced; there is a triangle of grass to the side of the road where several cars can park (SK072683). Walk back up the road for about a quarter of a mile beyond the cattle grid, and turn left along a gravel farm road. At the brow of the hill, turn left over a stile marked 'Concessionary path to Glutton Bridge via Chrome Hill' and follow the directions for the main route. When you reach the road after descending from Chrome Hill, turn left along it past Dowall Hall farm and up Dowel Dale to return to your car. This route is a little over 2½ miles but with a fair amount of ascent and descent, and includes a mile along a very quiet road. You can also reach this route from the bus stop at Glutton Bridge, which will add just over a mile of walking.

Amenities

There is no pub in Hollinsclough, but you will find several pubs and cafes in Longnor, two miles off. In the other direction, the Travellers Rest at Flash Bar may provide meals, though it was being refurbished when I last passed; if you turn left here and then shortly right into Flash village ('the highest village in England') you can eat at the New Inn.

The nearest public toilets are in Longnor, at the corner of the square.

Walk 25: Earl Sterndale and Dowel Dale

Start: the walk starts 4 miles SSE of Buxton on a minor road which links the B5053 at Earl Sterndale with the A53 near Cistern's Clough, 3 miles from Buxton. This is the road which passes the High Edge Raceway (stock car racing); it is very quiet except on race days. Park on the grass verge where a walled gravel track leaves the road on the south-west side (SK083678). This is about a quarter mile north-west of the B5053 and 200 yards south-east of Harley Grange, the only farm on this road.

You can also park on the verge near the point, halfway along the walk, where the route meets the same road (SK077689). This is near the highest point of the walk. Please do not park in Dowel Dale; there is a layby that will take two or three cars just before the stile where you leave the road, but cars parked here spoil a fine view. If you plan to take the extension to Earl Sterndale village you can park in the village street there.

Distance: 4 miles (alternatives 5 to 5½ miles).

Public transport: There is a bus route from Buxton to Longnor, with several buses each day, and this passes the Earl Sterndale crossroads.

This walk combines fine views of unspoilt White Peak landscape with contrasting views down into huge limestone quarries, and also takes you down a quiet dale. It is reasonable in wet weather although you will have to skirt a few muddy patches. We did this walk one New Year's day, after several days of freezing fog which had just cleared, and every tree and plant was coated with an inch of clear ice – a wonderful sight.

The walk is entirely in Derbyshire, on limestone. Half a mile is along very quiet lanes, and a further 200 yards or so along a B road. This does not carry a great deal of traffic.

The Walk

Walk south-eastwards along the road towards Earl Sterndale. At the crossroads, turn left and follow the road round a bend, then cross a stile on your right. Walk straight up the field, keeping to the left of the lime

Limestone rocks near Hindlow

kiln and aiming for a house. Cross the stile onto the lane and walk to the right for a few yards. You will find a stepped path on your left, just to the right of a magnificent rockery and looking as though it was part of the garden. Go up this path and over the stile at the top, then bear half-left up an obvious path. As the slope eases, follow the path as it bends to the right and leads straight up the slope to a stile. Cross this stile and look for another in the far left corner of the field, near what looks like a grey igloo. Over this stile, and you will find yourself on a straight trackway which follows the top of the ridge. Turn left along it.

You are now walking along the boundary of the Park. To your left is unspoilt countryside, with two jagged hills prominent in the view; these are Parkhouse Hill and Chrome Hill. To your right, in contrast, is an industrial scene; a vast and very active quarry, one of a line which caused this stretch of land to be left out of the Park. Blasting takes place here on most weekdays; the igloo is in fact a shelter, and you will see a notice advising you to take shelter if you hear the hooter which gives a few minutes warning. In fact the risk is small; you are unlikely to find any debris which has been thrown as far as this lane, but it is worth taking shelter until after the blast, just in case.

The track leads in half a mile to the main road. Cross it carefully and go through a stile nearly opposite. Follow a clear track, which bends

25. EARL STERNDALE AND DOWEL DALE

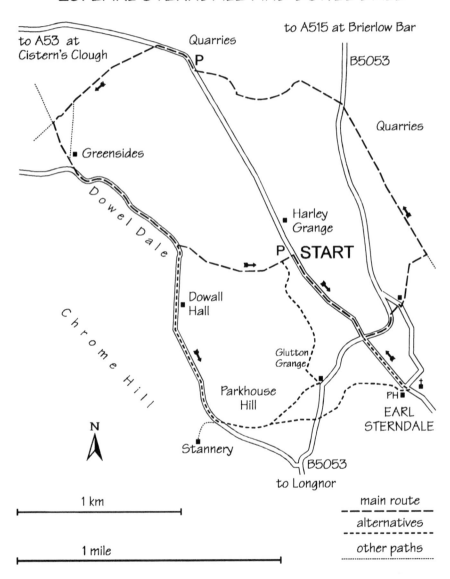

to A53 at Cistern's Clough

Quarries

P

to A515 at Brierlow Bar

B5053

Quarries

Greensides

Dowel Dale

Harley Grange

P START

Dowall Hall

Chrome Hill

Glutton Grange

Parkhouse Hill

PH

EARL STERNDALE

N

Stannery

B5053

to Longnor

1 km

1 mile

main route

alternatives

other paths

left to go through a gateway at the far end of the field. Once through this gate, branch right from the track and cross the field diagonally, keeping the hillock on your right, until a row of three gates comes in sight. Cross the stile beside the right-hand gate and follow the track onwards. It brings you to a byroad. Ignore the gate marked 'Bridle path' and turn right along the road. Watch out for a stile on the left in about a quarter of a mile, just before the brow of the hill, and just beyond an interesting row of weathered limestone rocks in the field on the left. This stile is not signed and is easily missed. Cross it and bear half-right across a field; the path is not clear, but you will soon come in sight of a wall with a corner towards you. Go left of this corner and follow the wall down the hill. Some of the many depressions in this field may be due to quarrying for walling stone, but most of them are probably swallow holes like the larger ones you will pass shortly.

Soon after Greensides farm comes in sight, cross a step stile and then continue alongside the wall. Just before the end of the field there is a wooden stile on your right; cross it and then turn left to continue following the wall, which is now on your left. You will shortly reach two footpath signs. Cross the stile on your left here and walk across the uneven field, aiming for the right-hand end of the belt of trees that shelter the farm. You will have to pick your way between some large depressions; these are 'swallow holes' where underlying caves in the limestone have fallen in. In wet weather you can see small streams running down the sides and sinking in the loose rock or vegetation at the bottom.

Join the lane at the same point as the farm drive, and walk left down the lane. A short way beyond a cattle grid, on your left, is a large natural pothole in the rock (the 'Owl Hole'); until recently this was used as a rubbish dump, but this is now prevented by barbed wire and banks which unfortunately make it difficult to see the pothole.

Continue along the lane down Dowel Dale, a small dry dale. Where the dale turns right in half a mile, go straight ahead across a stile. Climb the hillside, bearing slightly right up a faint path, and cross the stile at the top. Go straight across the field, heading towards Earl Sterndale which you can see in the distance. When you reach a gate, go through it and through another gate which you will find on your right. Turn left along a track which takes you down to the byroad where you started your walk.

Alternative route

You can extend the walk by about a mile, and take a look at Chrome

Hill and Parkhouse Hill, by remaining on the road down Dowel Dale instead of crossing the stile. The road passes Dowall Hall farm, opposite which a stream emerges from a small cave – this is probably the water that disappeared down the sink holes near Greensides. Below the farm the dale opens out as it joins the valley of the Dove.

Cross a cattle grid. Where a farm lane joins on the right, fork left along a well-trodden path which skirts round the foot of Parkhouse Hill, rising only slightly. This passes a rock marked with yellow paint, and then goes over a step stile by a wooden gate. A few yards on, by a small fenced plot, the path forks; take the clearer path, which goes straight ahead towards Glutton Grange farm. Beyond a waymarked gateway, aim for the right-hand end of a large farm building and go through the gate in the fence just beyond it. This brings you out by the farmhouse, a pleasant building dated 1675. Do not go through the gate to the road, but turn sharp left along a short lane with barns on its left.

At the end of this lane are several iron gates. Take the one on your right (marked with yellow paint) and go up the valley with the wall on your left. Continue over a difficult wooden stile beside a wired-up gate. A step stile brings you onto a walled track. Turn right, and you will be back at the road and your starting point in a few yards.

Another alternative, adding about 1½ miles to the main walk, takes you to Earl Sterndale and the 'Quiet Woman' inn. For this, follow the alternative route above, but after skirting the bottom of Parkhouse Hill fork right just past the wire-fenced plot. The path may not be visible on the ground, but you will see a wooden stile beside a gate at the bottom of the field, and another stile beyond which leads onto the road. Go straight across, and a clear path leads you steeply up the hillside through several stiles to emerge in the yard in front of the 'Quiet Woman'. Turn left along the road, and go straight across the crossroads, to return to your starting point.

Amenities

The 'Quiet Woman' in Earl Sterndale offered only sandwiches, not hot food, on my last visit. Unlike most Peak District pubs, this one appears to cater for local people (many of them quarrymen) as well as visitors; so don't monopolise the dominoes! Real Ale is on offer.

There are several pubs and cafes in Longnor, a mile and a half south along the B5053, and of course more in Buxton.

The nearest public toilets are at Longnor, in the square.

Walk 26: Sparklow and High Wheeldon

Start: Sparklow car park (SK128659) on the High Peak trail, a short way from the A515 Buxton to Ashbourne road.

The verge of the minor road between Hurdlow Town and Wheeldon Trees is wide, and you should have no difficulty in parking there (around SK110666) if you prefer. The road surface is poor in places.

Distance: 5 miles (alternative 6 miles).

Public transport: there are two or three buses a day (except Sunday) from Buxton to Monyash which pass the Duke of York at Pomeroy, 200 yards from the route, and the crossroads on the A515 a quarter of a mile from the car park. On Sundays there are buses from Sheffield and Chesterfield to Buxton, and also from Derby and Ashbourne to Buxton, which pass this crossroads – few in winter, more in summer.

This walk follows the most northerly part of the High Peak Trail, a former railway line, to its end north of Hurdlow. It then goes along a farm track and a footpath to Wheeldon Trees farm. From here you climb the prominent hill of High Wheeldon which belongs to the National Trust, a fine viewpoint. The return route is along a very quiet road through Hurdlow Town, which despite its name consists only of two or three farms. You pass relics of an earlier route of the old railway.

The walk is entirely in Derbyshire, on limestone. It should be reasonable whatever the weather. About two miles are along a very quiet minor road, with a wide grass verge for much of its length.

The Walk

Note that the sketch map is drawn with East at the top.

From the car park (formerly the goods yard of Hurdlow station), walk north along the High Peak trail under the bridge. The trail was originally the route of the Cromford and High Peak railway, opened in 1831, which linked the Cromford canal a couple of miles south of Cromford with the Peak Forest canal at Whaley bridge. This part of the line was later (in

26. SPARKLOW AND HIGH WHEELDON

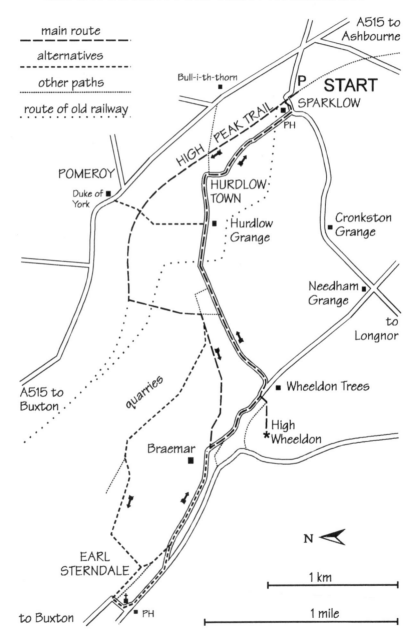

main route

alternatives

other paths

route of old railway

A515 to Ashbourne

Bull-i-th-thorn

P START

SPARKLOW

PH

HIGH PEAK TRAIL

POMEROY

Duke of York

HURDLOW TOWN

Hurdlow Grange

Cronkston Grange

Needham Grange

to Longnor

A515 to Buxton

quarries

Wheeldon Trees

High *Wheeldon

Braemar

N

EARL STERNDALE

to Buxton

PH

1 km

1 mile

1899) incorporated in the Ashbourne to Buxton railway, and many curves were eased and bridges widened at that time. The line was closed in 1967 as far as Dowlow quarry, and converted into an all-weather path for walkers, cyclists and horse riders. At Dowlow the line passes out of the National Park, and beyond this point it is still in use for mineral traffic from the great limestone quarries.

In a mile and a half you will reach a sign marking the end of the High Peak trail, at a point where a walled farm track crosses the route of the old railway. Turn left along this track (it may be muddy in places). In a couple of hundred yards, notice an overgrown walled track which crosses yours. This is not a farm track, but part of an earlier route of the railway – you will meet it again later. Continue straight on along your track, and in a quarter of a mile you will reach the brow of a hill. Fifty yards beyond this, half-way between two electricity poles, you will reach a pair of stiles – a squeezer on the left and a decrepit step stile (marked by yellow paint) on the right. Go over the stile on the right. (Other stiles on this path are also in poor condition, though passable. If you prefer you can continue down the track to a tarmac road and turn right for Wheeldon Trees farm; this will save you half a mile, but you will be returning by the same route).

There is no visible path across the field, but walk parallel with the wall on your right. At the far side of the field, near the top, is an iron gate; below it a stile with wooden steps and a board at the top of the wall (one of the alternative routes uses this); and below this again an inconspicuous step stile, which you should go over. Go diagonally across the next field to a wooden stile leading you into a belt of young trees, and a second leading you out of it, and head down the field aiming rather to the right of the nearest hill (High Wheeldon). Cross a poor step stile, then bear slightly more to the right. As you come over the curve of the field you will see a barn; your next stile is in the wall a few yards above it, by a waymark post. Beyond this turn left along a green track which curves right (passing a gate) to a wall gap and a wooden stile, with a waymark post by it. Over this, then cross a step stile halfway down the wall opposite and finally a step stile in the lower corner of the next field which brings you onto the road. Turn left along the road.

In a third of a mile, opposite a road forking left, is the entrance to Wheeldon Trees farm. Cross a stile on the right, go straight ahead over another stile and climb to the top of High Wheeldon, a conical limestone hill which belongs to the National Trust. There is a fine view across the valley of the Dove and you can see the tower of Longnor church showing over the ridge opposite, though most of the village is hidden. To the right is a range of prominent hills, ending with the craggy Parkhouse and Chrome hills, and beyond them and to the left the smooth ridge of Axe Edge. Here you are at the edge of the limestone; the range of hills from High Wheeldon to Chrome Hill is made of hard 'Reef limestone', representing the edge of an ancient sea, and the Dove valley in front of you is cut in the softer shale. Beyond this, forming Axe Edge and the hills in front of it, the rock is millstone grit, a form of sandstone.

Turn round and return to the road, and across it into the minor road which slants up the steep hillside and then turns left. Continue along the road, passing the end of the walled track from the High Peak trail. In another quarter mile, just past a bend in the road, you will cross the earlier route of the railway again, curving round the hillside to your right. This looks tempting, but it is not a right of way and is blocked by fences. However you can see from the road, here and further on, that the line is mostly level but ends in a straight incline (up which traffic was hauled by a stationary steam engine) running down to join the High Peak trail near to the bridge at Sparklow. The incline became unnecessary in the 1860s, when more powerful locomotives were available; so the section of line you recently walked along was built, on an acceptable gradient of 1 in 60, to replace the incline and part of the level line above it.

Shortly the road passes Hurdlow Town, which is simply a small group of farms including Hurdlow Grange and Hurdlow Hall. (Take a path on the left opposite the first farm if you want to return to the Duke of York at Pomeroy; at the High Peak trail go straight across). Some of these buildings are attractive to look at, but watch your step as the road here shows obvious signs of its use by livestock. Continue along the road; you will cross over the foot of the incline on the older railway route, about 200 yards short of the Royal Oak inn, and there is a good view of it from here. Turn left and go down a path on your left just beyond the inn, and the car park is on your right.

Alternative routes

You can add an interesting mile to the walk by following the ridge above Earl Sterndale. When you have walked up the farm track from the end of the High Peak trail and turned right across the field, go through the upper stile, nearest the iron gate, instead of the lower one. The path for half a mile beyond this point is not shown as a right of way on the map, but it is well used and the stiles are in good condition though old. Walk across the field with the wall on your left, and beyond the next stile you will have the wall still on your left and a wire fence on your right

Quarry above Earl Sterndale

separating you from a deep drop into a quarry (which now extends further than shown on the OS map). A notice warns you to keep out of the quarry, and a wooden shed provides shelter when blasting takes place. There may be blasting at any time between 8 am and 4 pm, Monday to Friday, and signs warn you that when you hear the hooter you have five minutes in which to reach the nearest shelter.

Just before the next shed, there is a stile on the left and the path continues as a walled track. To your right you look down into a huge active quarry, in total contrast to the rural landscape on your left.

In another quarter of a mile the path bends to the left at an old iron gate. Shortly it bends right again, and here you should leave it along the firm track which forks left and shortly turns left down the hill, with a fine view over Earl Sterndale village to the spiky Parkhouse and Chrome hills.

At a T junction turn left, and then left along the road to Wheeldon Trees, unless you want to look round Earl Sterndale village or visit the Quiet Woman inn. In that case (which involves an extra quarter mile) turn right, then at the road turn left past a rather attractive little school and the church which has been restored after bomb damage in the war,

An ancient lime kiln: a common sight in the Peak District

and the Quiet Woman is ahead of you. Turn left along the road, forking left past the village shop, to reach Wheeldon Trees in about a mile.

Amenities

The Royal Oak inn is just above the car park at the start of this walk. In Earl Sterndale is the Quiet Woman, a homely inn which (at least at my last visit) offers real ale and sandwiches but not hot food. Turning left out of the car park and following the major road brings you to the Packhorse inn before the bridge at Crowdecote in two miles. If you turn right out of the car park and left at the main road you will come to the Bull-i-th'-thorn hotel and the Duke of York inn. There are also inns and cafes in Buxton and Longnor.

There are picnic tables in the Sparklow car park.

The nearest public toilets are at Longnor (in the square) and at the Parsley Hay car park on the High Peak trail, two miles south.

Walk 27: Sheen and Hartington

Start: I suggest that you start the walk in Sheen, which is much quieter than Hartington, although it does mean that the last part of the walk is uphill. The village street is wide and straight so you can leave your car there (around SK111611) without causing an obstruction.

If you prefer you can start the walk in Hartington. Use the car park off the Hulme End and Warslow road, B5054, on the outskirts of the village; this may be full at summer weekends.

Distance: 3 miles (alternatives 4 to 6 miles).

Public transport: there is a regular, though not very frequent, bus service between Buxton and Hartington on Mondays to Saturdays, with occasional buses to Ashbourne and Leek. On Sundays, in summer only, there are two buses in each direction between Buxton and Ashbourne via Sheen and Hartington, and also ramblers' services to the Peak District, calling at Hartington, which leave towns including Huddersfield, Sheffield, Chesterfield, Mansfield and Derby in the morning and return in the evening. On Saturday there are occasional buses from Hanley to Hartington.

This walk descends from the village of Sheen, which is on a ridge between the Dove and Manifold valleys, and crosses the Dove to Hartington. It crosses the river again at Hartington Bridge, and climbs the ridge again to return to Sheen.

The Dove forms the boundary between Staffordshire and Derbyshire. This part of its valley lies on shale, which makes for smooth rounded contours and good soil; the walk therefore runs entirely through farmland. There may be muddy patches, though most of the walk is dry. About a mile of the walk is on a minor road.

Hartington is deservedly one of the show villages of the Peak, with its neat houses clustered around a village green and pond, and the church on the hillside behind. Unfortunately it is too popular for its own good, at least at summer weekends, when the village is clogged with parked cars and tourists and sometimes a fuming traffic jam. A large Stilton cheese factory is discreetly hidden down a cul-de-sac, and an excellent little shop by the pond sells cheese from the factory and elsewhere.

Beresford Dale

Sheen, in contrast, is rarely visited by tourists. There is a Victorian church but no shop, and one pub. The village straggles along a single street. As far as I know, its only claim to fame is that it was the last place visited by Nikolaus Pevsner in completing his fine series of books on 'The Buildings of England'.

The Walk

Walk along the only street of Sheen towards a group of buildings which includes the old village school and vicarage, a short way south of the church. Take a footpath just south of these buildings on the same side of the road. (There is an alternative path which starts a hundred yards further south, through the farmyard of Lower House, but this may be muddy). The beginning of your path is marked by a waymark post, which directs you down the gravel drive of a house set back from the road, but in fact the way is through a gap in the fence on the left immediately inside the gate, and then alongside the fence and down the field to a hidden stile at its lowest corner. Continue in roughly the same direction through several waymarked stiles. When you cross a stile just beyond a concrete track, do not go to a stile straight ahead of you on the skyline but bear slightly right (as indicated by the waymark)

27. SHEEN AND HARTINGTON

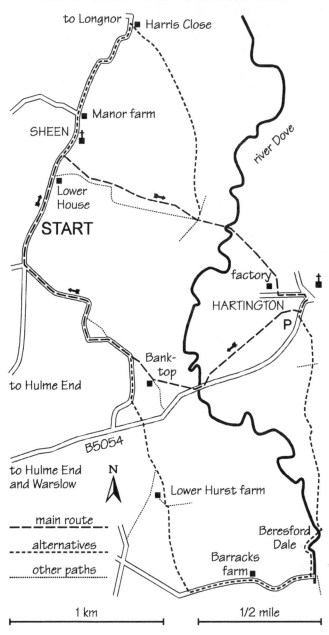

to Longnor — Harris Close

Manor farm

SHEEN

river Dove

Lower House

START

factory

HARTINGTON

P

Bank-top

to Hulme End

to Hulme End and Warslow

B5054

N

Lower Hurst farm

Beresford Dale

Barracks farm

main route

alternatives

other paths

1 km

1/2 mile

to a more prominent stile. The path descends a little valley. When you come to a farm lane, go straight across and over the stile opposite.

Go straight on across the field and you will reach a footbridge over the Dove. Beyond this an obvious path bears right and leads to the left of a large industrial building (the cheese factory) and joins its access road. Turn left along this into Hartington and you will soon come to the village green, with the cheese shop on your left and the church up a lane opposite. Turn right and right again (after exploring Hartington, if you wish) along the Warslow road. A short distance from the green you will see a pottery and the public toilets on your left, behind a small private parking area. (The public car park is a few yards further on, on the right). Almost opposite the pottery, just a few steps nearer the green, is an inconspicuous but elegant squeezer stile. Go through this, and follow the path between buildings and along the left side of a farmyard to a stile in the wall beyond. Cross it, and bear slightly left through a line of stiles, to reach the road again a short way before the bridge over the Dove. The building beside the bridge is Hartington Mill, now converted to a private house.

Go over the bridge carefully and cross a stile by a gate on the right. Walk up the sloping field and pass just to the right of a house; the right-of-way across the field is marked by white disks. The path comes out on a drive. Turn right along this and you will arrive at a minor road. Turn right, and then right again at a crossroads in about three quarters of a mile, to return to Sheen and your car.

Beresford Dale

Alternative routes

For a route which adds nearly a mile and some good views to the walk, go northwards straight along Sheen village street past the church instead of taking the path on the right. About half a mile beyond the church, the road swings off to the left at a point where there is a farm (Harris Close) on the right. Enter the farm drive, which has a footpath signpost, and then go to the right of all the buildings through a narrow gap between a barn and a wall. Continue in this direction through several stiles, keeping alongside the wall on your right.

At the highest point of the ridge, stop to admire the view. You are on gritstone here, as you can tell by the colour of the walls. To your right you look over Sheen and the valley of the Manifold to the gritstone moors of the Morridge. To your left the Dove valley is cut into the softer shale, and the hills beyond are obviously limestone. Ahead you can see Hartington village.

Beyond the next stile the wall on your right ends, but go straight ahead on a faint path which leads to the next stile, where the wall starts again; on your left is a steep slope into the Dove valley. The path runs through a plantation. Beyond it, leave the wall at last and go straight ahead, past a waymark post, onto a clear path which slopes down the hillside and comes out on a farm track.

Turn right along the track, and in a hundred yards look out for a footpath signpost and a pair of stiles on opposite sides of the track. Take the one on your left. Go straight across the field, over the footbridge, and follow the obvious footpath past the cheese factory – you are now back on the main route of the walk.

You can also extend the walk by two miles to include Beresford dale, which is short but very attractive, especially early in the year when there are drifts of snowdrops. This dale was a favourite haunt of Isaac Walton, author of 'The Compleat Angler', and his friend Charles Cotton who lived at Beresford Hall close by (but demolished many years ago). To take this route, instead of going through the stile opposite the pottery in Hartington, go up the path between the pottery and the public toilets and bear half-right. A well-worn path will lead you across fields and over a farm lane, and eventually into Beresford Dale. As you descend to the dale, you may be able to see through the trees on your right a small building; this is Charles Cotton's 'Fishing temple', but there is no public access to it. This and a tower on the hillside, together with an ornamental gateway on the main road, are all that remain of Beresford Hall.

Just beyond the footbridge is the 'Pike pool', named not for its fish but for the pike, or spike, of rock that rises from it. Where the dale opens out there is another footbridge, but do not cross it. Instead, walk up the tarmac road to your right. After half a mile, beyond a caravan site, you will find a footpath sign and a step stile on your right, at the end of a small belt of trees. Cross the stile and walk alongside the trees, over a very wet patch (see below if it is too wet to cross), then bear slightly right and make for the next belt of trees. You will find a stile just to the right of it, and the path runs just inside the tree belt, and then a short way across a field, to reach a tarmac farm road. Go left along this for a few yards, and then right through a squeezer stile opposite a pond. Follow the waymarked route alongside the farmyard fence and straight ahead over several fields until you reach the main road. Cross this and go through the stile opposite, and then up the hillside (bearing slightly left) to the far corner of the field. Here you join a minor road. Turn right along it. In a mile, turn right at a crossroads and you are back at Sheen village street and your car.

After wet weather you may baulk at the wet patch shortly after leaving the Beresford Dale road. If so, continue along the road, round a right-hand bend, and turn right at the crossroads. In 200 yards you will find a signpost, gate and stile on the right. Follow the waymarked path, eventually passing a tennis court and a farm on your right, and you will rejoin the original path shortly before it reaches the main road. This will have added a quarter of a mile to your walk.

Amenities

There are several pubs and cafes in Hartington village, all well used to catering for tourists and their families. If you prefer somewhere quieter, try the Greyhound at Warslow. And don't forget to stock up with cheese in Hartington!

There are toilets in Hartington village, by the pottery on the Warslow road.

Walk 28: Tissington and High Peak Trails

Start: the car park at the former Hartington station (SK149611), a mile and a half east of Hartington village on the B5054 road. There is a small charge at the car park, and there are toilets and a picnic area there.

You can also start this walk from the free car park at Friden (SK172607), or (at the cost of an extra half mile) at Parsley Hay car park (SK147638), for which there is a small charge. Parsley Hay car park gets very full at summer weekends; you are fairly sure to find space at the others. You can hire a bicycle at Parsley Hay if you want a change from walking.

Distance: 6 miles (alternative 4 miles).

Public transport: there is a regular, though not very frequent, bus service between Buxton and Hartington on Mondays to Saturdays, with occasional buses to Ashbourne and Leek. On Sundays, in summer only, there are two buses in each direction between Buxton and Ashbourne via Hartington, and also ramblers' services to the Peak District, calling at Hartington, which leave towns including Huddersfield, Sheffield, Chesterfield, Mansfield and Derby in the morning and return in the evening. On Saturday there are occasional buses from Hanley to Hartington.

This walk is an exception to the general rule that walks in this volume are 3 to 5 miles long; this one is 6 miles, although an alternative route shortens it to 4. However it is very easy walking, since most of it is along level trails (former railway lines) or level roads, so if you can manage five miles in open country you will find this walk is no greater effort than that. The short section of walk that is over fields is all downhill. (How do we manage that? The railway and road section is in fact uphill, though imperceptibly so).

The walk is entirely in Derbyshire, on limestone, and is satisfactory after wet weather. There may be mud in the farmyard where you leave the road, but you can avoid this by a short detour.

There is about half a mile of road walking; only a short part of this is on the main road, and there is an adequate verge. But watch out for silent cyclists on the trails!

For users of the Ordnance Survey 'Outdoor Leisure' map there is a minor problem; the route crosses the boundary between the front and back of this two-sided map. I suggest you fold your map so that the eastern half is accessible; this will cover two-thirds of the route. The rest of the walk is on the railway trails so you cannot get lost!

The Walk

From the Hartington station car park, walk past the old signal box and turn right along the Tissington Trail. This is an all-weather path for walkers, cyclists and horse riders, converted from the former railway line from Ashbourne to Buxton. It makes very easy walking, but watch out for cyclists coming up silently behind you – bells seem to be out of fashion.

The trail crosses the road on a high bridge and passes through the first of several cuttings. These are hewn out of the limestone rock and have an interesting flora, including cowslips in season – they serve as a linear nature reserve. Between cuttings there are impressive views to the left towards the Dove valley. After a mile and a half the trail joins another railway converted to a path, the High Peak Trail. This used to be the Cromford and High Peak railway, a very early line which ran over the Peak to join the Cromford canal at Cromford, south of Matlock, with the Peak Forest canal at Whaley Bridge a few miles south-east of Stockport. The centre section of it was taken over by the Ashbourne to Buxton line about 1900, but the eastern section survived until the 1960s. The history of the line is interesting, though I cannot discuss it here – there are several books about it. The old signal box at Hartington station car park is set out as a small information centre, open at weekends, where you can learn a little about the history of the trails.

Turn sharp right along the High Peak trail (unless you want to visit Parsley Hay car park, in which case go straight on for a quarter of a mile). You will notice that this railway was much narrower than the other, and as you go on you may also notice that it is made up of straight sections joined by sharp curves, instead of the sweeping curves of the Tissington trail. You will also notice a different surface underfoot – ashes rather than gravel – although this is gradually being replaced because it collects puddles in wet weather.

Shortly you pass through a short tunnel, the only one on the trail. Above each entrance you will see carved the crest of the railway company; the two carvings are different but both incorporate one of the

28. TISSINGTON AND HIGH PEAK TRAILS

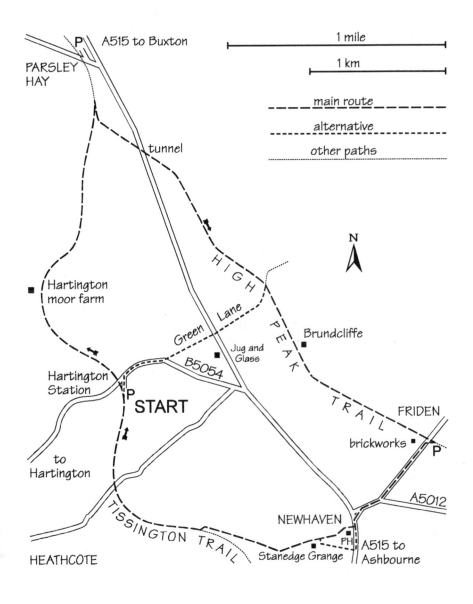

early railway waggons, designed to be pulled by horses rather than locomotives. You will also see the date, 1825.

Continue along the trail for another two miles to the car park and picnic site at Friden, just past a large factory which makes refractory bricks. Turn right beyond the bridge, and walk down to the road and turn left along it, past the factory. In a quarter of a mile bear right at the road junction; take care, because this is a main road, but there is a broad grass verge. At the next road junction, with a grass triangle, turn left towards Ashbourne.

A short way past the junction on the right you will see a farm and the Newhaven inn. Before you reach these, cross a stile on the right at a footpath sign just before the first farm building (not quite where it is shown on the OS map). Walk along the track and through the gate, and bear half-left to a stile at the end of the field (again not quite where the OS map suggests). Now aim to the right of the buildings ahead to another stile, cross a track, and go on through the stile opposite.

If the path I have described looks muddy there is a short diversion which avoids it. Do not cross the first stile but continue along the road past the inn and turn right along a firm farm road. In 200 yards, turn right along another track and look out for matching stiles in the walls on either side. Cross the one on your left and you are back on the main route.

Go straight on from this stile, across another stile, and join a track which leads through a gap in a belt of trees. Do not aim for the bridge ahead, since it is not easy to join the trail there, but bear well to the right across the field (no obvious path) and a stile half-way down the wall will come in sight. Cross this, and continue in the same direction to another stile, and then a third. Beyond this, steps lead you down to the Tissington Trail. Turn right along it, passing a picnic site on your right among newly-planted trees, and you will be back at your starting point in less than a mile.

Alternative routes

If you have the OS map you will see that there are several tracks and footpaths that you can use to vary this route. Longer walks would perhaps be outside the scope of this book, but you can easily shorten the walk to four miles. Start as described, but a mile beyond the tunnel turn right along a firm farm track which crosses the trail. Go straight across the main road, and on to join the B5054. Walk carefully down this for a quarter of a mile and the car park entrance is on your left.

Barn near Hartington

Amenities

As you leave the Hartington station car park, if you turn left Hartington village is a mile and a half on, and there are several inns and cafes there – also an excellent cheese shop (by the pond). Parking may be difficult, but there is a small car park just beyond the west end of the village on the right of the Warslow road, or you can park on the wide verge of this road.

If you turn right from the station car park you come shortly to the A515. Turn right for a mile to the Newhaven inn, or turn left for a short distance for the Jug and Glass. There is a restaurant by the filling station at the Newhaven road junction, but it does not appear to open at lunchtime.

There are public toilets in the car parks at Hartington station and Parsley Hay (but not at Friden), and in Hartington village near the car park.

Walk 29: Hall Dale and Milldale

Start: the car park (SK131557) in the village of Alstonefield, three miles south of Hartington. It may be full at summer weekends, but you should be able to park safely in the road nearby.

Alternatively you can use the car park (SK138548) at Milldale, on the Dove three-quarters of a mile south-west of Alstonefield; the car park is about 200 yards out of the village up a side valley (Hope Dale).

Distance: 4 miles (alternatives 2½ to 4½ miles).

Public transport: there are a very few buses from Ashbourne and Leek calling at Alstonefield on certain days of the week only. There are two buses between Ashbourne and Buxton on Saturdays; and on Sundays a Derby – Ashbourne – Buxton – Manchester bus calls at Alstonefield. On summer Sundays there is also a ramblers' bus from Mansfield and Derby, and one on alternate Sundays from Macclesfield.

This walk takes you from the attractive village of Alstonefield, past Stanshope Hall and down Hall Dale, one of the most attractive of the dry dales. The main route then takes you up the quiet side of the upper part of the Dovedale gorge. From the popular hamlet of Milldale you return to Alstonefield either by a very quiet byroad or across the fields.

The main walk is entirely in Staffordshire (the Dove forms the boundary), and on limestone. The most attractive stretch is on National Trust land. The route is impracticable after heavy rain, but an alternative can be followed in any weather although there may be muddy patches. Alstonefield is a complicated little village with several intersecting roads, so follow the instructions carefully as you leave and re-enter the village.

The Walk

Note that the scale of the sketch map is distorted at Alstonefield in order to show the way through the village more clearly.

Leave the car park by the track which leads from the back of the 'coaches' section to join a road in front of a telephone box. Turn right along the road, and straight on at the crossroads; at the next junction turn left, and then turn left again down a walled track. All this happens within a hundred yards, so don't walk too fast!

Where the track turns sharp right, go straight ahead through a stone squeezer stile by a gate, and down the field with the wall on your right. By a tree this continues into a narrow field; bear right to go over a squeezer stile by a narrow gate at the bottom of the field, and steeply down with the wall on your left into Hope Dale. The path turns right with the wall and leads through a squeezer stile onto a road at Dale Bottom.

Go straight across the road and up the walled track opposite. In half a mile this brings you to Stanshope, with its attractive 17th century brick and stone hall. At the little triangular green in front of the hall, turn left down a walled track signposted to Milldale. After a hundred yards go through a squeezer stile on the right, signposted to Dovedale, and in fifty yards over a stile in the wall on your left.

Make for another stile on your right, at the lowest point of the field, and continue beyond it down Hall Dale, going straight on at a waymark post and crossing several stiles. The dale becomes deeper and steeper, and beyond a bend there is a wood on the right. In May you will find

Hall Dale

29. HALL DALE AND MILLDALE

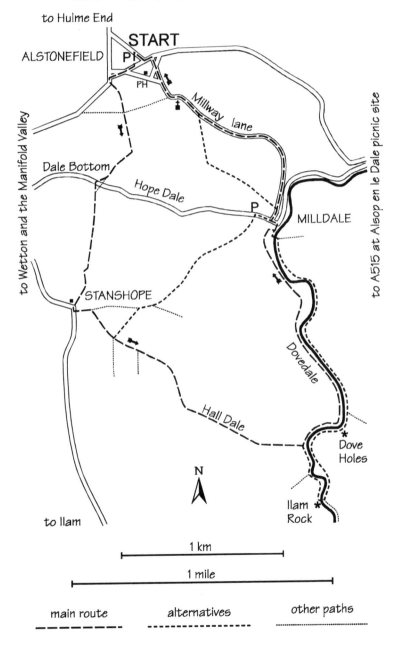

purple orchids on the grassy side of the dale. Eventually the dale meets Dovedale and you come out on the bank of the river.

Here your way is left along the riverbank. However the path from here to Milldale may be impassable if the river is high; you will not have to walk far to reach the section which is liable to flood. At any time the path is very rough in places and some of the stiles difficult. So you may prefer the alternative route, which is over the stile on your right.

The path upstream along the river is rough but very attractive; you can watch the crowds walking along the main Dovedale path on the far bank. This is very popular at summer weekends, and a firm all-weather path has had to be made the whole length of the dale to combat erosion. Your path is much quieter, perhaps because it is less easy. After following the river bank for about half a mile, past the twin caves of Dove Holes on the other side of the river, the path leaves the river bank. It slopes up the hillside over three stiles and to the right of a small barn. Beyond the barn the path is less obvious but continues in the same direction, climbing slightly, till it reaches a stile into a small wood. After the wood the path is clear as it runs across a hillside which is full of cowslips in the spring, with orchids and many other wild flowers as well.

Eventually you will find yourself on a knoll above Milldale village. The path descends very steeply over rocks to your right (there is a longer but less steep way to the left if you prefer). It comes out between buildings almost opposite the packhorse bridge made famous by Isaac Walton, whose 'Viator' dared cross it only on hands and knees! To be fair to him, the bridge has been widened and the parapets raised since packhorse days.

Turn left for a few yards to the road, cross it and go up a minor road opposite (Millway Lane), passing a house where refreshments are usually on sale and then a telephone box. You can continue up the steep and very quiet tarmac lane to Alstonefield, but if you prefer to cross the fields (the distance is much the same) you should climb the steps on the left immediately past the telephone box, at the footpath sign, and go very steeply up the fields with the wall on your left. When the slope eases you can see Alstonefield church in the trees ahead, and the row of stiles leads first slightly towards the left of the church and then to the right of it, rejoining Millway Lane a short way below the church.

Continue past the church gate to the road and go straight ahead between the village greens, leaving the George inn (and the post office tearoom beyond it) on your left. Turn left at the junction, and then right at the fork, to return to your starting point.

Alternative route

You can avoid the rough and possibly flooded path up the Staffordshire side of the Dove, and see a bit more of Dovedale, at the cost of an extra half mile or so. To do this, when you reach the river at the foot of Hall Dale turn right through a squeezer stile, and follow the riverside path. This used to be dreadfully muddy, but much work has been done recently to improve it. You will come to a footbridge over the Dove at the foot of the spectacular Ilam Rock. Cross the bridge into Derbyshire and turn left along the main valley path, which will bring you to Milldale over Viator's bridge.

For a shorter walk (2½ miles), park at Milldale and take the path signposted 'Stanshope' almost opposite the car park. As you approach Stanshope, look out for a path on the left which takes you down into Hall Dale, and turn left down the dale. Follow the main route, but when you reach Milldale turn left along the road to reach the car park.

Dovedale is deservedly the most famous of the 'Derbyshire Dales' (although one side of it is in Staffordshire!) and there are some excellent walks in and near it. The main valley path is crowded in summer but very pleasant on a frosty winter morning, but the rough path along the eastern rim of the dale is always quiet and has some spectacular views. However, the paths in the dale have been thoroughly covered in other books, perhaps best of all in Mark Richards' 'White Peak Walks – the Southern Dales'.

Amenities

The George inn at Alstonefield offers hot food every day. It gets crowded at summer weekends, in which case you may like to try the Royal Oak at Wetton, the Manifold Valley hotel at Hulme End or the Greyhound (one of my favourites) at Warslow. There is a cafe at the post office, near the George, in Alstonefield and another in Wetton, and light refreshments at Milldale. There are several inns and cafes in Hartington, although parking may be difficult there on a summer weekend.

There are public toilets at the car park in Alstonefield and also by the packhorse bridge at Milldale.

Walk 30: Coldwall Bridge and Okeover Park

Start: at Okeover bridge (SK163481), a few hundred yards west of the tiny church at Mapleton (or Mappleton – both spellings are used). Mapleton is a mile and a half north-west of Ashbourne and is reached by a minor road from the top of Ashbourne market place, passing the southern end of the Tissington trail. Turn left just beyond Mapleton church.

Parking near the bridge is very limited, though there is room for two or three cars. If you cannot find a safe space there, park near the church in Mapleton village; the road is straight and quiet, and not too narrow.

Distance: 4½ miles (alternative 3½ miles).

Map: the walk is not covered by the Ordnance Survey 'White Peak' Outdoor Leisure map, nor (apart from a short stretch) by the OS one-inch Peak District touring map. If you need a map it should be the 1:25000 Pathfinder sheet 810 (SK04/14), 'Ashbourne and the Churnet Valley', or the 1:50000 Landranger sheet 119, 'Buxton, Matlock and Dovedale'.

Public transport: there are a very few weekday buses from Ashbourne to Mapleton. On Saturdays there are three buses each way between Ashbourne and Ilam via Mapleton and Thorpe (you can rejoin the bus route by walking north from Coldwall Bridge). On Sundays there are buses from Nottingham, Derby and Ashbourne which call at Mapleton and Ilam, continuing to Buxton; only one each way in winter, more in summer.

This walk takes you alongside the lower reaches of the Dove, after it has emerged from the narrow limestone gorge of Dovedale into more open country. It crosses a remarkable bridge, visits the tiny hamlet of Blore, and returns through the parkland of Okeover Hall. Less than half of the walk is within the Peak Park, but it is too good to miss because of that! This is a grand walk at any season, but perhaps at its best in spring when the leaves are just starting to break on the trees.

The first half of the walk is in Derbyshire and the rest in Staffordshire; here, as for most of its course, the Dove forms the boundary. The walk is partly on limestone and partly on the red soil of the Triassic rocks.

Most of it is reasonably dry; some stretches will be muddy after rain, but not impassable if you are wearing boots. There is about half a mile of road walking, on very quiet roads.

The Walk

Note that the sketch map is drawn with East at the top.

From Okeover bridge, walk about 50 yards along the road towards the domed church at Mapleton and go over a wooden stile on your left (upstream). From here the path across the meadows follows the river for about two miles, through several stiles and gateways. As you walk, notice how the field boundaries on your side of the river change from hedges to limestone walls as you get into limestone country; across the river there are mainly hedges. Ahead of you, you will soon see the conical limestone hill of Thorpe Cloud.

At a stone squeezer stile by an electricity pole, the river makes a loop to the left while the path runs across the field; aim slightly right of Thorpe Cloud for a gap in the hedge where you rejoin the river. Beyond the next field a wooden footbridge marks your entry into the Peak Park. Further on, a slab bridge leads you into a patch of woodland (the OS map shows a branch path from here to Thorpe village, but it is not apparent on the ground). At the end of the wood is a muddy patch, which you can skirt to the right.

At the end of a long field the stile is a little further from the river. Follow the hedge on your right, through a field full of lambs in spring, to a gate between farm buildings. From here there is a clear track, leading through a gate and up to a junction with another track. Turn left here over Coldwall Bridge into Staffordshire, and out of the Peak Park.

If you have not been here before, you will be surprised to find that this rough track is carried across the Dove by a massive stone bridge and a long walled causeway; quite out of place on a farm track. The explanation is that the bridge was built, soon after 1762, as part of the Blythe Marsh to Thorpe turnpike road. This was to link Thorpe (which was on an existing turnpike) with what is now the junction of the A52 and A523 roads two miles west of here, and thence with the Potteries. This section fell into disuse, perhaps because the present route by Mayfield was more convenient, and ceased to be maintained as a turnpike in 1831; from Coldwall farm over this bridge to Thorpe the route is now only a farm track. There is a milestone (erected in 1822) a short way up the track towards Thorpe.

Coldwall Bridge

Near the end of the causeway there is a footpath signpost. Go straight ahead, even though no arm points that way – this is another of those annoying paths which is not marked as a footpath because it is legally a public road. Go straight up the field, or up the faint green track which curves round to your right, to a wooden stile in a wire fence on the skyline, rather to the right of Coldwall farm. You have a choice of rights of way here, but that through the farmyard may be unpleasant underfoot. So go over the stile and across the field. Aim between a clump of trees, just right of a dutch barn, and an isolated tree further right, and you will reach the road (and the Peak Park again) at a stile and footpath sign.

Turn right along the road, passing the attractive Blore Hall which has some details dating from around 1500; its farm buildings have been neatly converted into holiday cottages. Turn left at the crossroads, past the church. The lane dips to cross a dry valley – you are on limestone here. You can take a slightly shorter route across the fields by going through a squeezer stile, almost hidden in the hedge on the right, just beyond the vicarage drive, and rejoining the road at the dip; but the stile at the latter point seems to be missing and you may have to scramble over the fence. (On one occasion in summer I found the road flooded at the dip, so had to use this path). The lane shortly brings you to the

30. COLDWALL BRIDGE AND OKEOVER PARK

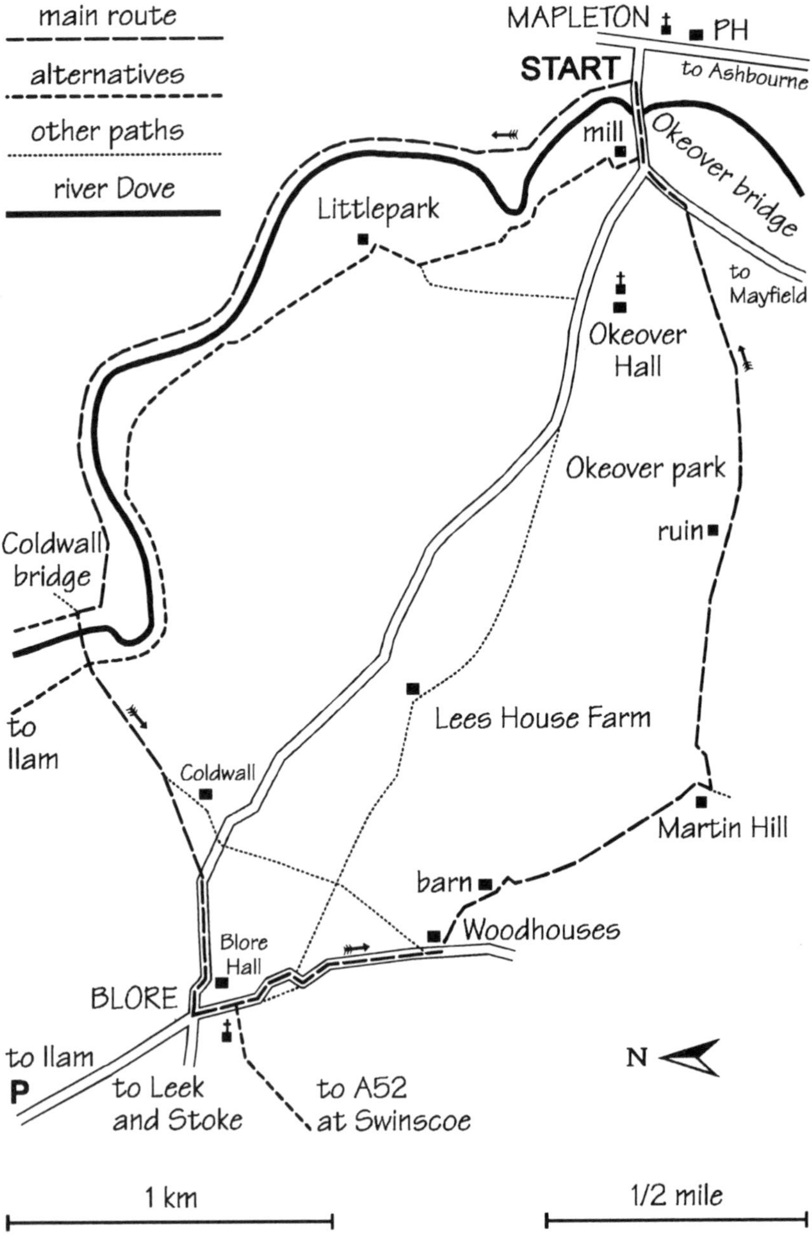

main route

alternatives

other paths

river Dove

MAPLETON

PH

START

to Ashbourne

mill

Okeover bridge

Littlepark

to Mayfield

Okeover Hall

Okeover park

ruin

Coldwall bridge

Lees House Farm

to Ilam

Coldwall

Martin Hill

barn

Woodhouses

Blore Hall

BLORE

to Ilam

P

to Leek and Stoke

to A52 at Swinscoe

N

1 km

1/2 mile

curiously designed Woodhouses farm, where you leave the Peak Park again.

Here the tarmac road bears right uphill, but you should go straight ahead, through a gate between the farm and another building, into a walled track. Beyond a barn you will have to make a short diversion, through an iron gate on your left, to avoid a barbed wire fence. Carry on parallel to the hedge on your right, through several gateways to one just left of an iron Dutch barn.

From this gateway you can take a short cut half-left, past a small building and derelict walls and hedges, but the right-of-way is along the obvious track, past the farmhouse, and then left just before a farm building on the left. An iron gate leads into a green walled track. Either way you come to a wooden stile. Go half-left to an isolated pair of stone gateposts; then turn half-right, past an ancient tree, and aim for a gate in the distance in the gap between two belts of trees. On the way there, and beyond it, the ground shows the 'ridge and furrow' pattern of medieval ploughing.

Beyond the gate you are in the tree-studded parkland of Okeover Hall. A faint green track leads to the right of a derelict house and down the hill, with the beginnings of a small valley to the right. Beyond a cluster of ancient trees, Okeover Hall comes in sight on your left. Part of the hall (and the impressive stable block behind it) is Georgian, the rest was built in matching style in the 1950s; the church beside it is medieval. The hall is still, I believe, the private residence of the Walker-Okeover family.

When you reach the unfenced tarmac road (not the hall drive) turn left along it, and you will come to a T junction where you leave Okeover park. To the left are impressive iron gates by Robert Bakewell of Derby, responsible for much fine ironwork, and ahead is a well-preserved watermill. Turn right along the road and you will be back at your starting point in a few hundred yards.

Alternative routes

You can save perhaps a mile, and most of the ascent and descent, by returning from Coldwall bridge along the west (Staffordshire) side of the Dove valley: but the way will be muddy in places after rain. To follow this route, turn left at the signpost near the end of the Coldwall bridge causeway. The path follows the river bank, becoming a muddy track where it enters a wood. It is waymarked through a long meadow to a stile beside a gate. A few yards beyond this, leave the riverside track at a waymarked stile on the right and follow a rather muddy path up through the wood, over a difficult stile, and straight on across the field. Beyond a waymarked stile, aim to the right of the buildings of Littlepark farm. Follow the fence on your left, and where it turns left (waymark) turn half-left to a stile which brings you out on the farm road at a footpath signpost.

Go right along the farm road for about 100 yards. Where it bears right, go over a stile in the hedge on the left and follow the visible green path half-right across the field, to cross a stile by a tree. The path goes over a small footbridge, follows the hedge on the left, and soon reaches the bank of the Dove, which it follows for a short way to a large weir. This supplies water to a mill, which you can see ahead. The path runs alongside the millstream, and through the yard to the right of the mill. At the road, turn left and you will soon reach your starting point at Okeover Bridge.

The OS map shows yet another possible route from Blore to Okeover, by way of Lees House Farm, and this is unobstructed; but it is little used and there is no visible path most of the way. It is less attractive than the routes described.

Amenities

The Okeover Arms inn at Mapleton is next door to the church; almost opposite, the village shop advertises cream teas. The Dog and Partridge is at Thorpe crossroads, half a mile east of Thorpe village, and there are several inns and cafes in Ashbourne. There are cafes, but no inn, in Ilam.

Blore Hall now houses a restaurant which offers bar lunches at prices which compete well with most pubs. Drinks with food only. The booted appear to be welcome. However, the 'traditional Sunday lunch' is often fully booked in summer.

The nearest public toilets to this route are in Thorpe village and at the Blore Pastures car park a quarter of a mile north of Blore crossroads.